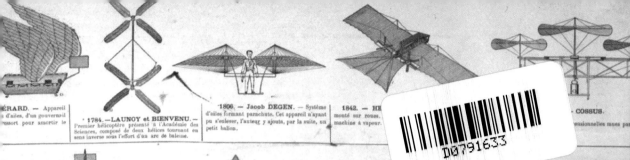

ÉRARD. — Appareil
d'ailes, d'un gouvernail
ressort pour amortir le

1784.—LAUNOY et BIENVENU. —
Premier hélicoptère présenté à l'Académie des
Sciences, composé de deux hélices tournant en
sens inverse sous l'effort d'un arc de baleine.

1806.— Jacob DEGEN. — Système
d'ailes formant parachute. Cet appareil n'ayant
pu s'enlever, l'auteur y ajouta, par la suite, un
petit ballon.

1842.— HE... ...
monté sur roues, ...
machine à vapeur. ...

COSSUS. ...
...asionnelles mues ...

1856. — Viscount CARLINGFORD.
— Genre d'aéroplane monté sur roues, possé-
dant une hélice et une queue mobile.

1857. — LE BRIS. — L'auteur produisait l'abaissement
des ailes à l'aide de leviers; des ressorts aidaient à les relever.

1857. — Du TEMPLE. — Disposition d'aéroplane monté sur roues, avec
une hélice à l'avant actionnée par la vapeur.

1859. — BRIGHT. — Syst...
d'hélices ascensionnelles tournan...
verse.

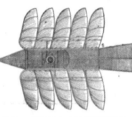

1864. — De GROOF. — Appareil composé
... mues par trois leviers, et dans lequel l'auteur
... la mort.

1864. — STRUVE et TELESCHEFF. —
Ailes mues par la force humaine agissant sur un
ressort.

1864. — CLAUDEL. — Aéro-
nef orthoptère. Système d'ailes tour-
nantes actionnées par la vapeur.

1866. — BOURGART. — Appareil mû
par les pieds. Dans cette disposition, l'aile se
présente en tranchant pendant son relèvement, et
à plat pendant son abaissement.

1867. — Le BRIS. — Les ailes so...
leur orientation convenable force l'appar...

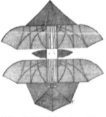

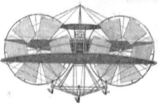

— Appareil mû par la va...
...ont basés sur le principe

1871. — DANJARD. — Appareil formant
parachute composé de deux ailes propulsives et
d'une hélice, le tout mû par la force humaine.

1871. — POMÈS et de la PAUZE. — Appareil pourvu d'un gouvernail et d'une hélice actionnée
par un moteur à poudre.

1871. — Thomas MOY. — Système d'aéroplane monté
sur roues et dont les hélices sont mises en mouvement par une
machine à vapeur.

1871.— PÉNAUD. — Premier
teur, dit planophore, composé de plans à b...
d'une hélice mue par la torsion du caoutch...
reil, qui peut monter ou descendre suivan...
son centre de gravité, a pu franchir 60 m. ...

...CH. — Machine volante composée d'une hélice d'ascension, d'une d'o-
...ail. La vapeur qui fait mouvoir les hélices agit directement sur ces der...

1876. — PÉNAUD et GAUCHOT. — Système d'aéroplane à vapeur
pourvu d'hélices, d'un gouvernail et de roulettes à pattes flexibles.

1877. — E. DIEUAIDE. — Expérience sur l'hélice au
moyen d'un tube flexible amenant la vapeur d'une chaudière
fixe. L'hélice double ne paraît pas susceptible, à cause de la
perte due aux engrenages, d'une force ascensionnelle de plus
de 12 kilogrammes par cheval-vapeur.

1877.— MÉLIKO...
coptère à vapeur d'éthe...
disposée pour former p...

1879. — BREAREY. — Système d'ailes flexibles mues par la
vapeur. L'appareil est monté sur roues, et son centre de gravité est variable pour l'ascension ou la descente.

1879. — TATIN. — Aéroplane à air com-
primé monté sur roues et expérimenté à Meudon.
A une vitesse de 8 mètres par seconde, cet appa-

1879. — DANDRIEUX. — Appareil disposé pour obtenir
un allègement sur place. Les ailes se meuvent suivant un axe oblique,
et le mouvement qu'elles font est à peu près celui du chiffre 8.

1880. — EDISON. — Projet d'un
...aécoptère étant la force du mou...

THE WRONG STUFF?

Attempts at Flight Before (& After) the Wright Brothers

Phil Scott

BARNES & NOBLE

NEW YORK

This edition published by Barnes & Noble, Inc., by
Arrangement with Hylas Publishing

2006 Barnes & Noble Books

Text Copyright © Phil Scott
Compilation Copyright © 2003 Hylas Publishing

M 10 9 8 7 6 5 4 3 2 1

ISBN 0-7607-77977-7

Printed and bound in China

The Smithsonian Institution is the world's largest museum complex and research
organization. Composed of 16 museums, archives, libraries and research facilities,
and the National Zoo, the Smithsonian's exhibitions offer visitors a glimpse into
its vast collection numbering over 142 million objects.

The National Air and Space Museum Archives supports the mission of the National
Air and Space Museum by acquiring and preserving for public and curatorial use
documentary materials of air and space flight. These documentary materials span the
history of flight from ancient times to the present day and comprise approximately
10,000 cubic feet of material including an estimated 1.7 million photographs,
700,000 feet of motion picture film, and 2 million technical drawings.

THE
WRONG
STUFF?

Phil Scott

Convair XFY-1 Pogo

TABLE OF CONTENTS

Twin-ski configuration of
the Convair XF2Y-1 Seadart

TO DAD

"They all laughed at Wilbur and his brother,
When they said that man could fly...
But oh-ho, who's got the last laugh now?"

—George Gershwin

INTRODUCTION

For most of history–until the Wright brothers came along a century ago–people didn't have a clue how to fly. But still they tried, God love 'em. Before the nineteenth century most folks figured that imitating birds was the way to go. Hey, it worked for the birds. A few intrepid aeronauts tried jumping off cliffs dressed as birds, but they ended up dead or crippled, depending on how far they dropped. Then they figured that if they captured a bunch of birds and hooked them up to some device they could fly around carrying a man.

A few built odd-looking wing flappers, or ornithopters as they came to be called. Some consisted of two rods held over the flier's shoulders and tied to his feet. Each rod came tipped with hinged wings that would open when the rod descended and close when it ascended. It didn't work. One man even tied wings to his arms and legs and jumped into the river Seine in Paris, but he only got hurt and wet. A lot of these ornithopters had two circular wings that manually flapped up and down simultaneously, but that didn't do much except make the inventors' arms tired.

One guy named Jacob Dengen gave it a try around the turn of the nineteenth century and actually succeeded in rising. He also had a balloon attached to his ornithopter, of course. But by the nineteenth century inventors started getting the basic airplane shape down, at least down to the wings and fuselage. And maybe the flying machine had some kind of tail. Or maybe it had only wings and a tail. It was so hard to decide. Most used a steam engine, just because it was tried and true. So what if it was way too heavy and put out too little power for the job? A few more used no engine at all, trying to glide down hills and such. They had, after all, learned from the earlier aeronauts that cliffs were just too dangerous. But sometimes the inventor forgot or was completely unaware of the lesson of dangerous cliffs.

Inevitably his glider was too fragile and its wings folded in mid-flight. Others had built theirs with such a high center of gravity that despite taking off from a hill the glider ended nosing up, falling on its tail and killing them in the crash. None had wing surfaces that controlled its roll.

And then came the Wright brothers.

The brothers (below) figured out that a flying machine needed a pilot with full control over the machine, and a machine that would allow itself to be completely controlled. Their wing-warping biplane, the Flyer, was the first powered airplane that allowed the pilot to control the craft's yaw, pitch and roll, its movements along the three axes of rotation–lateral, longitudinal and vertical. They flew it four times at Kitty Hawk on December 17, 1903, in a 21-mph wind. Their next machine, built the following year, they tried to fly in their hometown of Dayton.

Comte de Puiseux's
Flying Bicycle

The Zerbe Multiplane,
(see pp 48-49)

It didn't work very well and so the brothers had to figure out why. And when they did (not enough power, so it needed a catapult to launch it; plus it was too short to remain longitudinally stable) they built the first real airplane, the 1905 Flyer III. The Age of Flight had begun.

The brothers' aeronautical contemporaries, however, did not have the benefit of their wisdom. Because the Wrights wanted to protect their invention by securing patents for it around the world, they initially kept their mastery of powered flight a secret. That left other designers of the day to proceed from intuition, guesses, aesthetic judgment, trust in engine power—everything but the theory of three-axis control. The Wrights made their first public demonstration of powered flight in 1908, at an Army Signal Corps field in Virginia. A few competing concepts faded away after that, yet many designers thought they could improve upon the miracle, even though they were not as careful engineers as the Wrights. In fact, they may

As time went by, aeronautical engineers learned flight's secrets. But as aircraft became more specialized the engineers also wanted to solve the problems that erupted: building an airplane with a better view; dealing with vertical takeoff and landing; making and protecting the long-range bomber; guiding a missile with a poor guidance system; even—yes—finding an easier way for the pilot to commit suicide. Despite all the knowledge engineers had obtained, aeronautical engineering was still a black science.

In the last quarter of the twentieth century engineers had the aid of computer programs that built and tested simulated machines, and now the odd duck has become an endangered species. (Aircraft still fail spectacularly: There's the Marine Corps V-22 tilt-rotor, for instance, that kept on crashing and crashing.) You can be sure, though, that in a garage somewhere someone is working on a strange bird. He has barely more than a little learning and big dreams. That, after all, is what makes flying magic.

–Phil Scott

In the statistics I have included only the categories available to me. For instance I am aware of no data describing the length or height of Cayley's glider, nor of its speed. For such omissions I apologize.

not have been engineers at all. They might not have realized that a canard airplane worked best with a front wheel, say. Or they might have tried round wings, wings that formed a square, or an artistic design of tubular steel that held the whole machine together. And they certainly were not tied down by gasoline engines running propellers. They tried a crude jet engine, or even pedal power. Either way whatever they tried didn't work well. One guy, for instance, had a lot of success with three wings, so the manufacturer moved the cockpit forward and tried adding two more wings in back, and flew it once before having it disassembled rapidly. Others built huge aircraft with several wings, but those usually broke apart in the middle or rolled over and nosed into the ground. There just wasn't much research going on in the problems of aerodynamics.

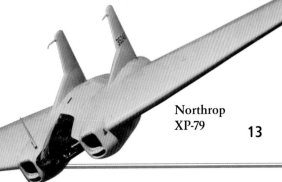

Northrop
XP-79

13

Three-quarter right front view, of a monoplane glider in low-level flight: possibly the Le Bris 1868 Glider, although the photograph appears to be from a much later date, possibly circa 1905

DA VINCI'S GREAT BIRD

He Was a Better Painter

One of the world's earliest, greatest minds to work on the aviation problem was no doubt Leonardo da Vinci. Instead of considering straight-winged flight like most of the 19th century inventors beginning with Sir George Cayley, da Vinci thought the best way to fly in the air was by imitating birds flapping their wings. Ornithopters, we call them now. The concept today seems strange, but 500 years ago man only knew one animal that flew: birds In 1505 he wrote, "In order to fly a bird uses its wings in the same way a swimmer moves his arms and legs." Okay, so he was wrong on that point. In brief, a bird flies more like it's doing the breast stroke. And its largest muscles are in its breast. Now da Vinci knew that part, and he also knew that a human's largest muscles are in his legs. So he designed his great bird to be driven by human leg

LEONARDO DA VINCI

While painting *The Last Supper* da Vinci hired a serene, beautiful man to pose for Jesus, and paid him well in gold. Then for Judas he went to the bars and there found a drunk with the perfect, haggard face. "I've posed for you before," the man told him. "I was Jesus."

Da Vinci's Great Bird

Weight: 540 lbs.
Engine: human legs

power—the legs would flap the wings. Then, once it took off, the arms and straps attached to his head would steer and control everything. He designed it to have a birch frame tied together with leather thongs; its wings were to be covered with starched linen fabric. Of course it only weighed around 500 pounds, which was a little much to expect a 160-pound man to lift onto his back and take off with it by jumping over a cliff. But in his aeronautical notebook, filled with 500 sketches of flying machines and 35,000 words describing how to build and fly them, he did advise "trial of the machine over water, so that if you fall you do not do yourself any harm." After his death that same notebook went to the library of a friend and was soon lost, and remained undiscovered until the time of Napoleon.

Model of da Vinci's Great Bird

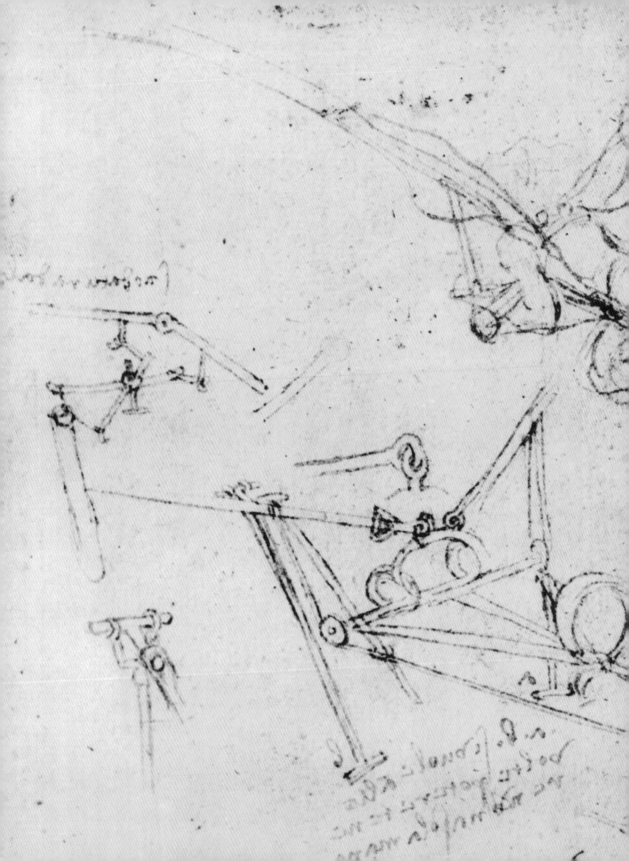

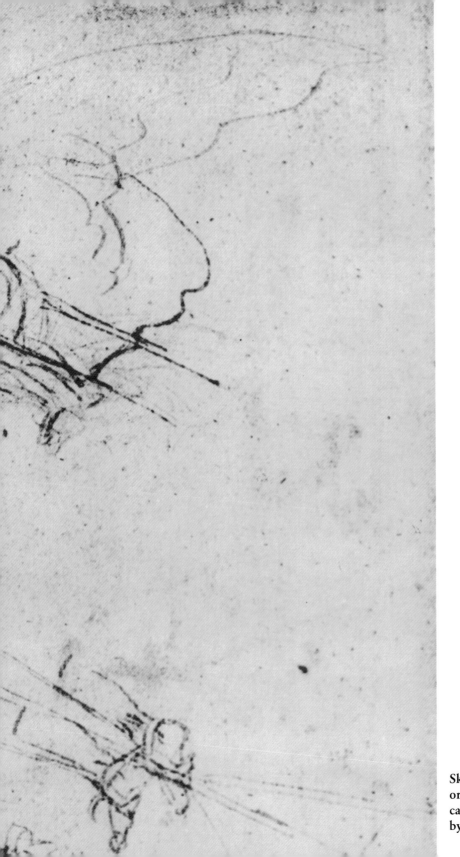

Sketch of a man-powered
ornithopter and mechni-
cal wing study drawing
by da Vinci ca. 1500

HENSON'S AERIAL STEAM CARRIAGE

Stock Option

In 1842 30-year-old British engineer William Henson filed a patent application for a "Locomotive Apparatus for Air, Land and Water," which, the application went on to describe, was "for conveying letters, goods and passengers from place to place through the air...." This "Locomotive Apparatus" was going to be one huge beast. Henson planned on it having a 4,500 square-foot, rectangular wing (140 feet long by 32 feet wide), covered top and bottom by either canvas or oiled silk. Its design called for three longitudinal spars running the length of the wing, and 26 wooden ribs to give it shape. The spars probably couldn't hold that kind of weight so the wing was braced with a series of wires attached at the wingtips and running over pylons—like a suspension bridge. It would have a steam engine of 25 to 30 horsepower buried in the fuselage and driving two pusher propellers (the first time propellers were designed for a flying machine) with six blades each. Its tail resembled a swallow's. All

together he estimated it would weigh 3,000 pounds, have a top speed of 50 miles per hour and a range of 500 miles. He figured it would cost 2,000 pounds (around three thousand dollars) to build and test the machine, so to raise this small fortune Henson formed the Aerial Transit Company and tried to sell 20 shares of stock for 100 pounds each. Unlike the Tulip Mania or the Internet Bubble no one rushed out to buy Henson's stock. Unable to build a flying machine Henson ended up patenting a safety razor, getting married, and moving to America to tinker with steam engines. But he never worked on another flying machine. Still, Henson's Aerial Carriage did resemble the modern airplane, and his innovative wing bracing was a precursor to later, more successful aeronauts.

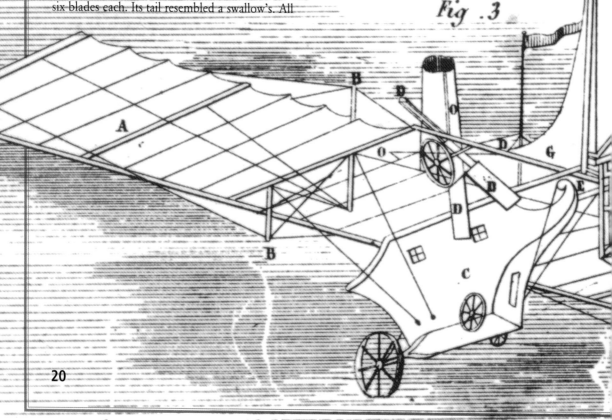

Fig .3

WILLIAM HENSON

"[We] are compelled, by careful inquiry, to profess our belief...that the earlier, if not immediate, possession of the long-coveted power of flight may now be safely anticipated."–*The Times of London*

Henson's Aerial Steam Carriage
Wingspan: 140 ft. long; 32 ft. wide.
Weight: 3,000 lbs.
Engine: 25-horsepower steam, turning two six-blade fans
Airframe: wood, covered with oiled silk or canvas

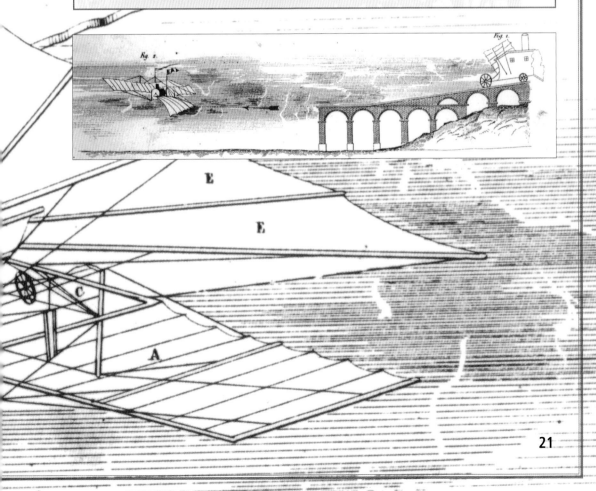

LE BRIS ALBATROSS

Rime of the Ancient Aircraft

French sea captain Jean-Marie Le Bris marveled at the sight of albatrosses effortlessly flitting above his ship, so he ignored the warning from the *Rime of the Ancient Mariner*. As he later wrote, "I took the wing of the [expired] albatross and exposed it to the breeze; and lo! in spite of me it drew forward into the wind; notwithstanding my resistance it tended to rise. Thus I had discovered the secret of the bird!" Upon returning to France, Le Bris constructed what was essentially an albatross big enough to hold a man. It was just over 13 feet long and had a 50-foot wingspan. There was no undercarriage– just a canoe-shape wooden hull where Le Bris intended to stand while piloting the glider. "An ingenious arrangement...worked by two powerful levers, imparted a rotary motion to the front edge of the wings, and also permitted their adjustments to various angles of incidence with the wind," Octave Chanute wrote in his seminal work, *Progress in Flying Machines*. These controls apparently were to have provided pitch control. Le Bris also designed a hinged tail for steering, both vertically and horizontally.

The good captain attempted his first flight in 1857. He tied the albatross to a horse-drawn cart; when the driver urged the horse into a gallop Le Bris untied the knot and the albatross leapt skyward, lifted by its wings. Unfortunately the rope wound itself around the cart's driver and pulled him into the air. Le

Bris managed to gently lower the driver to the ground unhurt, but he also crumpled a wing. On his next attempt, which he made from the edge of a precipice, "the apparatus...oscillated upward," wrote Chanute, "and then took a second downward dip..." Man and machine plunged to the bottom of the pit, breaking Le Bris' leg and destroying the albatross.

By 1867 he had completed another albatross much like the first, though a bit lighter and with a counterweight inside that was supposed to move automatically to provide equilibrium. If the craft pitched downward, for instance, the counterweight was supposed to slide backward to compensate. That was how Le Bris and others thought birds steered themselves. On the glider's first and only manned flight Le Bris rose to an altitude of perhaps 35 feet and covered perhaps 75 feet across the ground. The crowd that assembled

watched the whole flight and skewered Le Bris. It was hardly the kind of flight they expected from a real albatross. During one unmanned flight, performed away from public eyes, the glider rose nearly 80 feet in the air and flew nearly 600 feet before it settled back to the ground. On its final flight, again conducted away from the public, the glider rose from a hill and slammed nose-down into the ground, smashing it into little pieces. Luckily for Le Bris he was flying the albatross as a kite.

After that Le Bris gave up gliders for good. Broke, and ridiculed by the French, he returned home and soon enlisted in the 1870 French-Prussian War. We are told that he served with distinction. And if Chanute's account is true, the

Albatross was the first enclosed glider to actually fly. But on the whole the captain failed to solve the problem of longitudinal equilibrium—along with lift and drag.

JEAN-MARIE LE BRIS

"Le Bris had made a very earnest, and upon the whole, a fairly intelligent effort to compass sailing flight by imitating birds."
—Octave Chanute

"And I had done a hellish thing, / And it would work 'em woe: / For all averred, I had killed the bird / That made the breeze to blow."

Le Bris Albatross

Wingspan: 50 ft. **Length:** 13 ft. 6 in.
Weight: 92 lbs. **Engine:** none
Airframe: wood and fabric

Nyet Much

Ask any American who was the first to fly and unless they're into conspiracy theories they'll more than likely tell you the Wright Brothers. But ask any proud Russian and they'll give you a whole different answer: Alexander Mozhaiski, they'll say, and he did it nearly 20 years earlier, in 1884. A captain in the Imperial Russian Navy, Mozhaiski in 1881 designed a monoplane with a single steam engine that drove three propellers: one in the nose and two half-buried in the broad, rectangular wing.

Finishing it in three years, he asked for volunteers and a man named Goluber raised his hand. They took it to Krasnoye Selo, outside St. Petersburg, and set it up on a ramp. With Goluber behind the controls the monoplane rolled down the ramp and leapt about 100 feet uncontrollably.

And so the Russians claim that they were first, forgetting that an uncontrolled flight is just as good as no flight at all.

ALEXANDER MOZHAISKI

Alexander Fyodorovich Mozhaisky was born on March 9, 1825, in what is now Kotka, Finland. The son of a naval officer, he himself joined the navy and served from 1841 to 1862. Not getting enough of naval life, he also served from 1879 to 1882. Mozhaisky died in Saint Petersburg on March 20, 1890.

CLEMENT ADER'S ÉOLE AND AVION III

To the Batplane, Robin!

Clement Ader's aircraft owed their shape to the bat. And because bats don't need tails Ader found very little use for one either. But he must have believed storage was important, because his first flying machine, the Éole, could fan-fold its graceful 46-foot wings.

The craft was supposed to make its maiden flight in 1890 over the secluded Parc d'Armainvillers grounds in France, powered by a 20-horsepower steam engine. "An area was laid out in a straight line unturfed, beaten and leveled with a roller, Ader wrote six years later, "so that one could see and record the traces of the wheels from the slightest lift to complete takeoff." The ride was a wild one: 164

uncontrolled, erratic feet from start to finish, wavering just a few feet off the ground.

Ader convinced the French War Ministry that he could build a bigger and better Éole, and nearly six years later he finished the Avion III. It was powered by two steam engines (since the Éole's single steamer created destabilizing torque), and it had a wingspan of 52 feet. Much like Éole and a bat the Avion III was all wing and no tail. Ader sat behind the engines without a clear view of what lay ahead, though he did have some control over the wings. Hand cranks could change their angle of incidence—but they cranked a little too slowly to do much good.

Did the Avion III actually fly? Ader claims it did, but some historians doubt it. Here's the story according to *The Road to Kitty Hawk* by Valerie Moolman: In 1897, with two generals looking on at the circular track at Camp Satory near Versailles, Ader climbed into the machine, started its engines and took off with the wind blowing from behind. The machine was suddenly airborne, and Ader, fighting to stay inside the track's perimeter, steered to the left. But the wind blew his craft to the right. Ader chopped the power and the machine came down hard. It's not clear whether the machine had been propelled by the engines or the wind. In any case the generals departed to give their report to the War Ministry. And the Avion III? It was so damaged that Ader postponed further tests indefinitely, and the Ministry halted funding for good.

Years later Wilbur Wright hailed Ader as a pioneer of flight, but as the brothers' patent battle (in which they said they were the first to fly) heated up enough to melt steel, he wrote a letter to the editor of *Aircraft* magazine in 1910 to clarify his position. "[T]he Ader machine had...quite failed to solve the problem of equilibrium," he said. And also its pilot had made the grievous error of trying to take off downwind. Even bats know better than that.

Avion III

CLEMENT ADER
Clement Ader's Éole [1890]
Wingspan: 46 ft.
Weight: 727 lbs.
Engine: Ader-built 2-cylinder steam engine weighing 200 lbs.

Avion III [1897]
Wingspan: 52 ft.
Weight: 881.85 lbs.
Length: 52.5 ft.
Engine: two Ader 20-horsepower steam engines

MILLER FLYING MACHINE

Miller's Crossing

Sometime in the early 1890's, in Fairmont, (outside of Eugene) Oregon, George Miller put out a shingle that said "Flying Machines Made Here." And to prove it to anyone who happened to ask, Miller would show off a clockwork-powered helicopter model that could rise 30 feet in the air before running out of time. He got the idea for his machine as a 15-year old while driving his dad's harvester on the farm. "As I watched the rotating wings, I realized that I had before me an example of the mechanism needed for a flying machine," he said. Ten years later he had his four-wing model complete; instead of a small antitorque rotor he had two of them spinning in opposite directions from above. Now ready to build a full-size machine he decided to construct two sets of biplane wings, each set made from bamboo and silk. In case of power loss he knew they would rotate and allow the machine to float to the ground-- an early conceptualization of auto-rotation. Now all he needed was a lightweight engine. While he waited he received a patent in 1892, but in 1897 he got gold rush fever and joined his brother, poet Joaquin Miller, in Alaska. That wasn't the last of George Miller. "Have been studying on a new airship plane with new-old motive…" he wrote in his diary in 1923, at the age of 70. "The coming airship will need no engine nor gasoline, but will be propelled by power similar to that which lifts the sky rocket from the ground." So along with predicting autorotation he also foresaw the hypersonic scramjet.

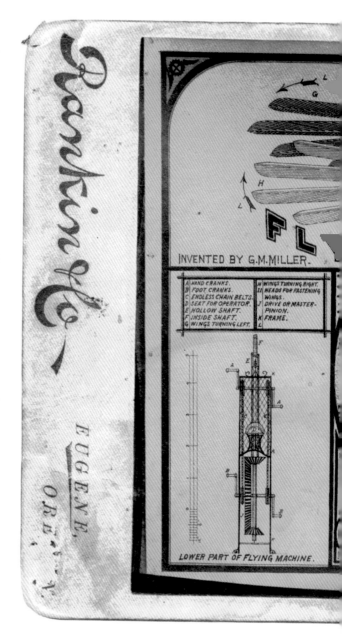

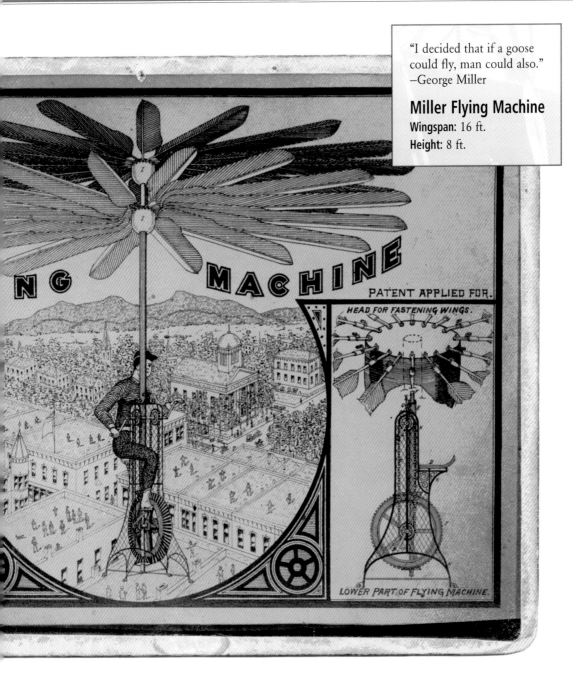

Miller Flying Machine
Wingspan: 16 ft.
Height: 8 ft.

An annotated patent drawing illustrating the human-powered Flying Machine designed by George Melvin Miller of Eugene, Oregon, in 1892. The helicopter-like design used hand cranks and foot pedals moved by the operator to turn two large coaxial counter-rotating propellers (at top) fitted with feather-shaped wings made of silk and bamboo.

29

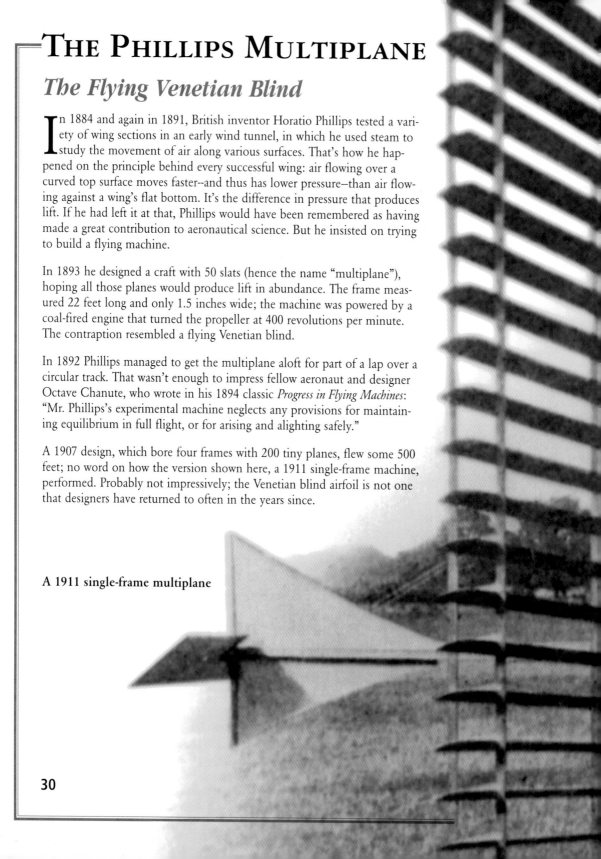

THE PHILLIPS MULTIPLANE

The Flying Venetian Blind

In 1884 and again in 1891, British inventor Horatio Phillips tested a variety of wing sections in an early wind tunnel, in which he used steam to study the movement of air along various surfaces. That's how he happened on the principle behind every successful wing: air flowing over a curved top surface moves faster--and thus has lower pressure—than air flowing against a wing's flat bottom. It's the difference in pressure that produces lift. If he had left it at that, Phillips would have been remembered as having made a great contribution to aeronautical science. But he insisted on trying to build a flying machine.

In 1893 he designed a craft with 50 slats (hence the name "multiplane"), hoping all those planes would produce lift in abundance. The frame measured 22 feet long and only 1.5 inches wide; the machine was powered by a coal-fired engine that turned the propeller at 400 revolutions per minute. The contraption resembled a flying Venetian blind.

In 1892 Phillips managed to get the multiplane aloft for part of a lap over a circular track. That wasn't enough to impress fellow aeronaut and designer Octave Chanute, who wrote in his 1894 classic *Progress in Flying Machines*: "Mr. Phillips's experimental machine neglects any provisions for maintaining equilibrium in full flight, or for arising and alighting safely."

A 1907 design, which bore four frames with 200 tiny planes, flew some 500 feet; no word on how the version shown here, a 1911 single-frame machine, performed. Probably not impressively; the Venetian blind airfoil is not one that designers have returned to often in the years since.

A 1911 single-frame multiplane

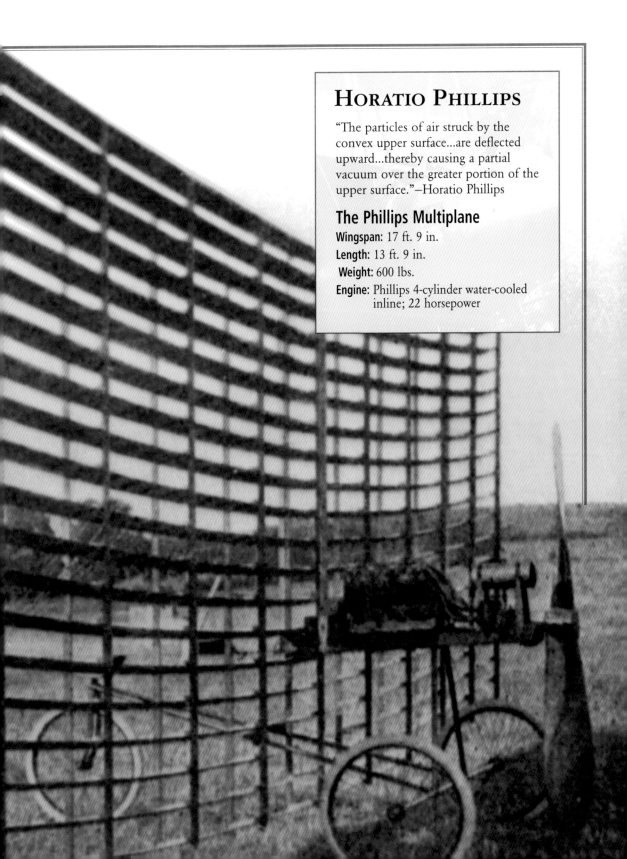

HORATIO PHILLIPS

"The particles of air struck by the convex upper surface...are deflected upward...thereby causing a partial vacuum over the greater portion of the upper surface."—Horatio Phillips

The Phillips Multiplane

Wingspan: 17 ft. 9 in.
Length: 13 ft. 9 in.
Weight: 600 lbs.
Engine: Phillips 4-cylinder water-cooled inline; 22 horsepower

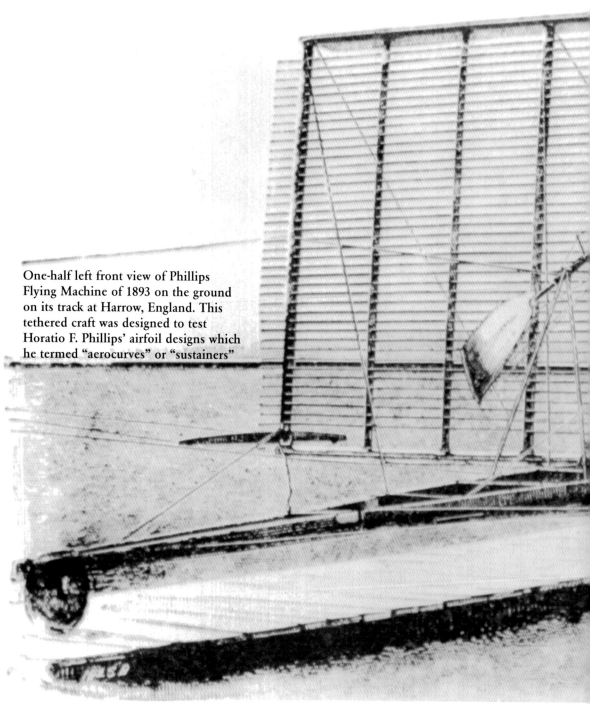

One-half left front view of Phillips Flying Machine of 1893 on the ground on its track at Harrow, England. This tethered craft was designed to test Horatio F. Phillips' airfoil designs which he termed "aerocurves" or "sustainers"

MAXIM'S KITE

The Great Kite o' War

In 1894 Sir Hiram Maxim put the finishing touches on his first and only aerial masterpiece. He called it the "kite of war." It was a huge biplane with some 4,000 square feet of wing surface and weighing in at an astounding four tons. Maxim gave it two steam engines, one on the right and one on the left, because he had this theory about flight control. You could steer a machine to the left or the right, he believed, "by running one of the propellers faster than the other." The differences in thrust would yaw the aircraft.

On July 31 of that year Maxim prepared to test the great kite in front of a journalist. He had constructed a track with an iron rail on which the machine's four wheels would sit. The vehicle was to take off down the track like a winged sled; as it gained speed the crew would attempt to raise it off the rail by using its "fore and aft horizontal rudders." As a safety measure the track had a wooden guardrail placed above the metal track, which would keep the kite from climbing way high.

With three crewmen aboard, the machine sped down the rail and lurched upward, skidding along on that upper wooden guardrail. But then it kept on going, until it had snapped right through the guardrail. A nervous Maxim quickly cut power and the kite settled down, one of its propellers cracking when it hit the guardrail. That flight ended before Maxim could even begin to test his theory about steering.

"Maxim spent 30,000 pounds, and his contribution to aviation was virtually nil," according to Peter Almond, author of 1997's *Aviation: The Early Years.* "I took a slightly generous view of him because of the sheer chronology. He did this in 1894, before anyone else had done any of it." And, generously, Maxim had something with his form of control. Around a century later desperate pilots attempting to land a crippled airliner in Sioux City, Iowa, used propulsion control after an engine explosion severed the hydraulics lines activating the aircraft's control surfaces. A few years later former astronaut Gordon Fullerton tested a computerized propulsion control system on a jetliner, and landed it safely. The time simply had not arrived for Maxim's use of divergent engine thrust.

Hiram Maxim

Hiram Maxim was an American inventor living in Britain who gave us a telegraph, several systems of lighting and more than 260 other inventions. Among other things he invented the Maxim Machine Gun. His purpose: to reduce the pain and suffering of war. He was as successful at that as he was at building airplanes.

Maxim's Kite
Wingspan: 104 ft.
Length: 145 ft.
Weight: 7,900 lbs.
Engine: 2 Maxim-designed 180-horsepower steam engines

WHITEHEAD NO. 21

Did He or Didn't He?

Gustave Whitehead lived near Berlin in the late 1800s and got to witness Otto Lilienthal gliding from his man-made hill outside the city. When he moved to Connecticut, at the turn of the century, Whitehead built a machine with bird-like wings covered with fabric, and a 12-horsepower engine weighing just 54 pounds and driving two propellers. On August 14, 1901, Whitehead said he made a few flights from a field near Bridgeport—one of nearly 1.5 miles that reached 200 feet. It being dark there were no photographs taken, and oddly enough he never flew again. But he talked about it so much that the anti-Wright contingent points to the Whitehead machine and maintain that it flew first. But the Wrights have that famous picture. Where's the Whitehead photo?

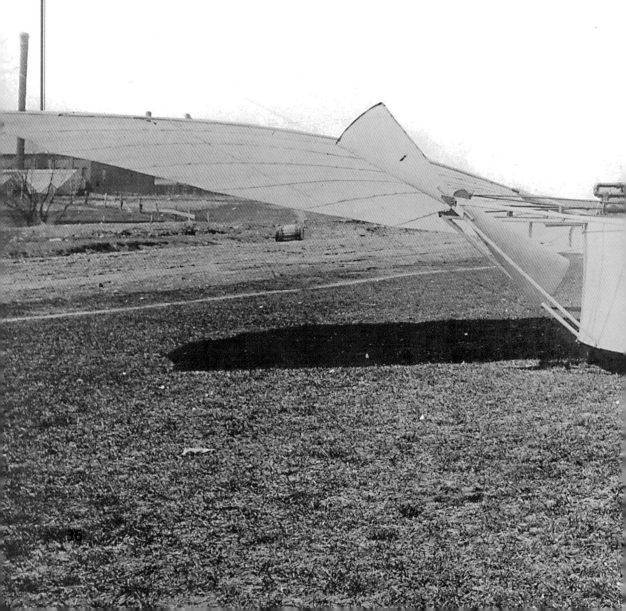

Reverse view of the Whitehead No. 21

Whitehead No. 21
Wing: bamboo, covered with 450 sq. ft. of silk
Engine: 12-horsepower

KRESS TRIPLE TANDEM SEAPLANE

The Early Poseidon Adventure

Austrian Wilhelm Kress was an inventor who started his aeronautical experiments in 1877. He worked his way up to rubber-band powered models, then in 1898 leapt to building a full-size flying machine. The machine, he figured, would be easier to fly from a lake, seeing as how it would be gentler on the body than the mountains of Austria. He finished it in three years–1901–two years before the Wright Brothers' Flyer. It had three wings placed in tandem above a canoe-shape fuselage. On its second wing he put twin pusher-propellers driven by a 24-horsepower Daimler engine. Its cruciform tail consisted of elevators and rudders. The 68-year-old Kress wanted to test his life's work himself, so in

October he took it to Lake Tullnerbach, outside Vienna, and sat it in the water. Then he sat in its cockpit and started the engine. The machine did move across the water some, but when he tried to turn the machine–still on the water, mind you–it rolled over and sank faster than the *Bismark*. Some say the engine weighed too much and sat too high, others say the float lacked a "step" to help it break from the water's surface like most modern seaplanes. Either way, it had no provisions for roll control like the technique of wingwarping used by the Wrights, nor were its wings structurally sound for flight. And that was the final voyage of the Kress Seaplane.

WILHELM KRESS

Kress Triple Tandem Seaplane (1901)

Wing Area: 366 sq. ft.
Engine: Daimler 24-horsepower

LANGLEY AERODROME

A Mud Duck

The success of the Smithsonian's Secretary Samuel Langley's unmanned Aerodrome 5, which flew a distance of 3,000 feet above the Potomac in 1896, encouraged him to start building a man-carrying version. He called it the Great Aerodrome. Langley applied for and received funding from Congress to the tune of $50,000. (President McKinley thought such an aerodrome would make a great observation machine for the Spanish-American War.) By 1902 it was finished—years behind schedule and long after America won the war. Langley even had to divert $23,000 from Smithsonian funds to complete it. The Aerodrome had a few problems, like wing ribs and a battery ruined by the dampness of the Potomac River and propellers that cracked when the engine ran for the first time. But by

October 7, 1903, the great machine was finally ready for its maiden voyage. Workers loaded the Great Aerodrome onto its houseboat catapult and the boat plowed to the center of the Potomac. Charles Manly, Langley's pilot, crawled into the small, cloth-covered car slung beneath the great machine, and in a few minutes the catapult kicked the Great Aerodrome down the 85-foot-long launch rail. When it reached the end it headed straight for the Potomac. They dried the Aerodrome and tried again, this time on December 8. Again the catapult shot it down the rail, but this time it slid tail-first into the now-icy river. Manly survived, Smithsonian boat crews tore the machine in two, and the following year Congress refused to allocate further funding.

46

Professor Samuel Langley

"[If] it is to cost us $73,000 to construct a mud duck that will not fly 50 feet, how much is it going to cost to construct a real flying machine?"
–Representative Gilbert Hitchcock, Neb.

Langley Aerodrome

Wingspan: 48 ft. 11 in.
Wing Area: 1,040 sq. ft.
Engine: One 52-horsepower five-cylinder water-cooled Balzer and Company radial

Langley Aerodrome 'A' on top of launching
house boat in the Potomac River.

THE WRIGHT 1904 FLYER

Flyer May Not Have Been the Wright Term

As just about everyone now holds true, the Wright brothers, Wilbur and Orville, receive credit for the first controlled, powered, sustained flight with their 1903 Flyer. All go and no show, on December 17, 1903 they flew it four times at Kitty Hawk, North Carolina, in a 27 mile-per-hour wind before a group of men who worked at a nearby lifesaving station. The wind caught it after the fourth flight and wrecked it, so the brothers packed it up and returned home with it.

The following year they built a virtual duplicate and tried to fly it outside their hometown of Dayton, Ohio. Like its predecessor, the 1904 Flyer was an airplane only the Wrights could love. With a wingspan of 40 feet and a length of 21 feet, it was squat and ugly; the twin-plane elevator was in front, its rudder was in back, and the pilot lay in the open on a cradle that controlled wingwarping on the lower wing. And he lay next to the gasoline engine. That engine powered two large pusher props that barely missed the sticks holding on the aft rudder. As for the wings, they sagged under their own weight and were built from pine, which tended to shatter after

a hard landing. Of which there were many. Though they'd built the launch rail four times as long as the one in Kitty Hawk from which it took off, there wasn't enough wind in Dayton to get it airborne. Despite that on May 23 they decided to demonstrate the machine to the press. About 12 reporters showed up on this windless day and got to watch the machine run down the rail and plop off the end without rising a single inch. The brothers invited them all back the next day and three made it. This time the machine actually flew—between 20 and 60 feet, depending on whose account you read. Then it crashed. The reporters left them alone after that. Flying as much as possible the whole summer Wilbur and Orville logged only 45 minutes in the air. When it did get airborne the machine would barely turn, or keep turning when it should have flown straight. The following year they built a machine that was longer, more stable, had a more powerful engine, and could fly with stability. And that, the 1905 machine, was probably the first real airplane.

ORVILLE & WILBUR WRIGHT

The Wrights built some 19 aircraft, most with the two-stick-and-no-rudder configuration. According to Wilbur, "An apt man, one who is quick at picking up things, can easily learn to fly in two hours." Today it takes a minimum of 40 hours. Wilbur died in 1912; Orville in 1948.

The Wright 1904 Flyer

Wingspan: 40 ft. 4 in.
Length: 21 ft. 1 in.
Max Weight: 900 lb. with pilot and 90 lb. of iron bars
Engine: 4-cylinder aircooled inline; 12-to 16-horsepower
Airframe: pine, muslin covering

Wilbur and Orville Wright at Huffman
Prairie, Dayton, Ohio, May 1904

47

ZERBE MULTIPLANE

Failure is an Option

History hasn't remembered Jerome Zerbe very well, except that he was an instructor at the Polytechnic High School somewhere in California in 1910. That year he designed and built his Multiplane, an aircraft whose five wing stepped upward as they came forward on the frame. It rested on three wheels and appeared to have a single engine, which drove two propellers. Zerbe took it to the Dominguez Air Meet, the first air show in the United States. It didn't fare too well, according to press reports. A few years later he resurfaced in Arkansas with the Zerbe Air Sedan. It, too, never flew.

JEROME ZERBE

"Tuesday, January 11th, 1910–Professor J. S. Zerbe brought out his curious appearing multi-plane and attempted to take off. As it clattered down the field amid the cheers of the crowd a front wheel hit a hole and collapsed throwing the machine to one side and damaging a wing..."
–Dominguez Air Meet by H.H. Hatfield

BLÉRIOT NO. V.

The Canard Without a Nosewheel

Louis Blériot seemed determined to fly by any means necessary. By 1905 he decided that the canard layout was the fashion to follow. And that's how he constructed his No. V. A single-wing airplane, it rested on two wheels beneath its center of gravity and one bolted beneath its tail. Its pusher engine was placed just before the vertical rudder, presumably for faster turns. To control ascent or descent Blériot incorporated weight shifting via a sliding seat. Moving forward pushed the nose down,

etc. On its first flight in September 1907 the engine died at an altitude of around 80 feet and the craft dived canard-first. The quick thinking Blériot jumped back behind the seat to restore its balance; the craft righted just before hitting the ground. And that was the final flight for Blériot No. V. Six models later Blériot finally hit upon the right combination of airframe, power and reliability. In his 1909 Blériot XI the Frenchman flew long-distance across the English Channel. Finally, Europe caught the Wright brothers.

Louis Blériot

From his system of numbering his aircraft it's evident that Louis Blériot tried, tried, and tried again. Finally he went on to fly his very successful No. XI monoplane across the English Channel in 1909.

Blériot No. V.
Wingspan: 25 ft. 7 in.
Length: 27 ft. 10 in.
Max. Weight: 572 lbs.
Engine: 24-horsepower Antoinette

ALBERTO SANTOS-DUMONT'S 14 BIS

The Airplane that was Built Backwards

Alberto Santos-Dumont, the son of a wealthy Brazilian, used his father's money to experiment with dirigibles and the like. Following the lead of Gabriel Voisin, who in July 1905 managed to get towed aloft in a glider dragged by a racing boat, Santos-Dumont envisioned one of his dirigibles, No. 14, lifting an aircraft, the Bis. (In French bis means "II" or "second." Take your pick.) Not one to be too involved in machinery, Santos-Dumont had his mechanics build a light frame of pine and bamboo, with wings that swept way upward. This effect, dihedral, would produce a natural stability. At the forward end was a boxy elevator, and on the other end was a four-blade propeller and engine built by a French company called Antoinette. It looked almost like an ordinary modern airplane, except built backward. The engine was a pusher, the tail went first, and the pilot stood facing it with a steering wheel in hand. Santos-Dumont thought it looked like a bird of prey. Everyone else thought it looked like a scared duck fleeing for its life. And so they called it a "canard." That's French for "duck."

In September 1906 Santos-Dumont installed an engine powerful enough to keep from launching it from the floating dirigible. On its first flight, the plane hopped anywhere from 23 to 43 feet—eyewitness accounts vary. The next month, before a crowd that included members of the Federation Aeronautique Internationale (formed the prior year to record aeronautical records) Santos-Dumont stood at the controls, poured on the power, and lifted off. He flew 197 feet before touching back down. That was the first official airplane flight in Europe.

To everyone except the Wright brothers. "If he had gone more than 300 ft. he has really done something; less than this is nothing," Wilbur wrote Octave Chanute. Wilbur seemed to forget that the first flight credited to humans, by his brother Orville on December 17, 1903, was but 120 feet in length.

Though Santos-Dumont devised an elevator similar to the Wrights', in general the designers "didn't develop [14 bis] in the same way the Wrights developed theirs, based upon lift and drag," says National Air and Space Museum curator Peter Jakob. "That's the thing that separates the Wrights. The Flyer was truly an engineered aircraft."

Santos-Dumont was back in the air in 1909 at the Reims Meet in France, the first air show in history. This time he flew his *Demoiselle*, a tractor monoplane that flew more like the Wright machines. It set no records, however. Suffering from multiple sclerosis, Santos-Dumont committed suicide in 1932 at the age of 59.

ALBERT SANTOS DUMONT

14 bis (1906)

Wingspan: 36 ft. 9 in.
Length: 31 ft. 10 in.
Weight: 661 lbs.
Speed: 25 m.p.h.
Engine: Antoinette 8-cylinder inline V; 50-horsepower
Airframe: pine, bamboo, cotton covering

Vuia No. 1

Acid-washed Genes

This early aircraft, completed in 1906, was the very first built with a tractor propeller—that is, a prop mounted in the nose. Designed and built by Romanian Trajan Vuia (who converted to French citizenship), the Vuia aircraft was a monoplane with a bat-like wing that could change its angle like a modern airplane's elevator. From tip to toe the frame below contained the engine, the pilot's seat and a rudder. The whole machine sat on four tires, the front two of which the pilot could steer. It was first tested in March 1906, then in July and twice that August. Witnesses said it could go about 80 feet in the air. On its final flight it crashed and was damaged beyond repair. Vuia never built another one. Instead, he worked for Allied forces during WWI with the French Ministry of Defense, and along with Victor Tatin builds torpedos for the military navy.

Vuia No. 1 (1906)
Wingspan: 28 ft. 6.5 in.
Length: 9 ft. 10 in.
Height: 10 ft. 9 in.
Weight: 531 lbs.
Engine: 25-horsepower Serpollet carbonic acid gas engine

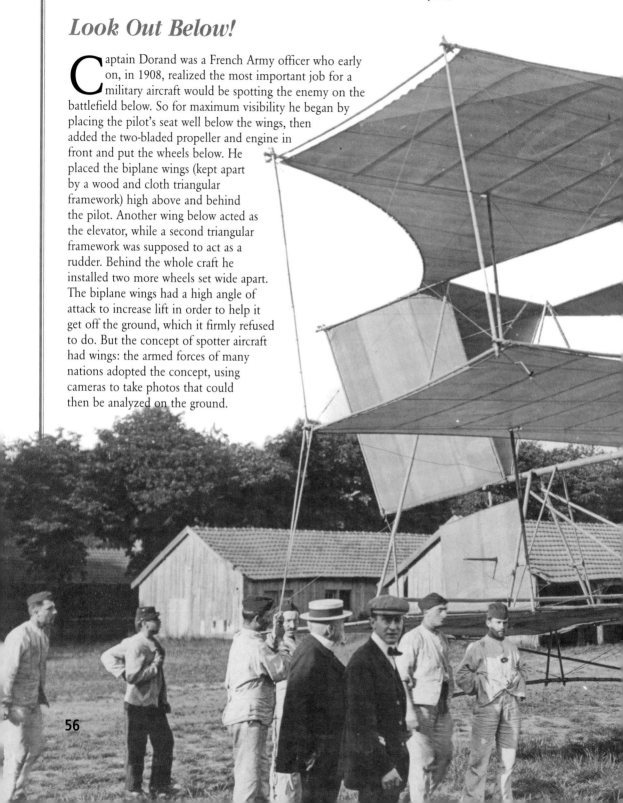

DORAND AEROPLANE

Look Out Below!

Captain Dorand was a French Army officer who early on, in 1908, realized the most important job for a military aircraft would be spotting the enemy on the battlefield below. So for maximum visibility he began by placing the pilot's seat well below the wings, then added the two-bladed propeller and engine in front and put the wheels below. He placed the biplane wings (kept apart by a wood and cloth triangular framework) high above and behind the pilot. Another wing below acted as the elevator, while a second triangular framework was supposed to act as a rudder. Behind the whole craft he installed two more wheels set wide apart. The biplane wings had a high angle of attack to increase lift in order to help it get off the ground, which it firmly refused to do. But the concept of spotter aircraft had wings: the armed forces of many nations adopted the concept, using cameras to take photos that could then be analyzed on the ground.

Dorand Aeroplane [1908]
Wingspan: 37 ft. 8.75 in.
Weight: 611 lbs.
Engine: Anzani 43-horsepower
6-cylinder air-cooled radial
Airframe: Wood and metal tubing
with fabric covering

Dorand aeroplane modified 1909

ALEXANDER GRAHAM BELL'S CYGNET

A Swan that Grew into an Ugly Duckling

Bell grew interested in flying machines watching his pal Samuel Langley experimenting with the series of Aerodromes back in the later years of the 19th century. He even snapped a picture of a miniature Aerodrome as it shot off Langley's catapult houseboat. In 1907 Bell formed the Aerial Experiment Association with a handful of young men, including Glenn Curtiss. Their intent: To get off the ground as soon as possible.

Bell was a big believer in kites built with the four-side triangular cell known as the tetrahedron. Such a cell, he wrote, possesses "qualities of strength and lightness in an extraordinary degree. It is not simply braced in two directions in space like a triangle, but in three directions like a solid…" Using hundreds of fabric tetrahedrons, he constructed a series of huge aircraft that he called Cygnets. That's French for "swans." Bell's swans, unfortunately, had no tails.

In 1907 AEA member Thomas Selfridge flew the first tetrahedron kite from Bras d'Or Lake near Bell's summer home in Nova Scotia. The Cygnet, with no controls, and Selfridge were towed behind a steamer. Once the aircraft alighted the steamer kept on steaming, dragging the poor Cygnet apart. Within two years Bell completed a second Cygnet, named, oddly enough, Cygnet II. From the edge it had a triangular wing, and it rested on runners. The pilot sat behind a biplane elevator and in front of a pusher engine with a 10-foot propeller. Despite three trials on the frozen lake that February, the Cygnet II remained firmly glued to the ice. The culprit seemed to be drag. The rest of the AEA members, including Glenn Curtiss, stuck to the pusher biplane that resembled the Wright brothers'.

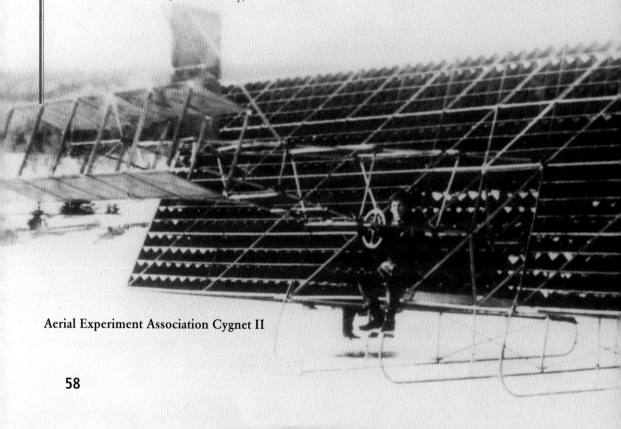

Aerial Experiment Association Cygnet II

ALEXANDER GRAHAM BELL

The first successful voice transmission over Alexander Graham Bell's telephone took place in Boston on March 10, 1876. His assistant, upstairs, heard Bell say, "Mr. Watson, come here. I want you." Bell had spilled acid upon himself.

Cygnet II (1908)

Wingspan: 42 ft. 6 in.
Length: 13 ft. 1 in.
Max Weight: 615 lbs.
Engine: Curtiss air-cooled 8-cylinder inline; 50-horsepower
Airframe: metal tubing, wood, cloth covering

D'EQUEVILLEY MULTIPLANE

A Well-Rounded Airplane

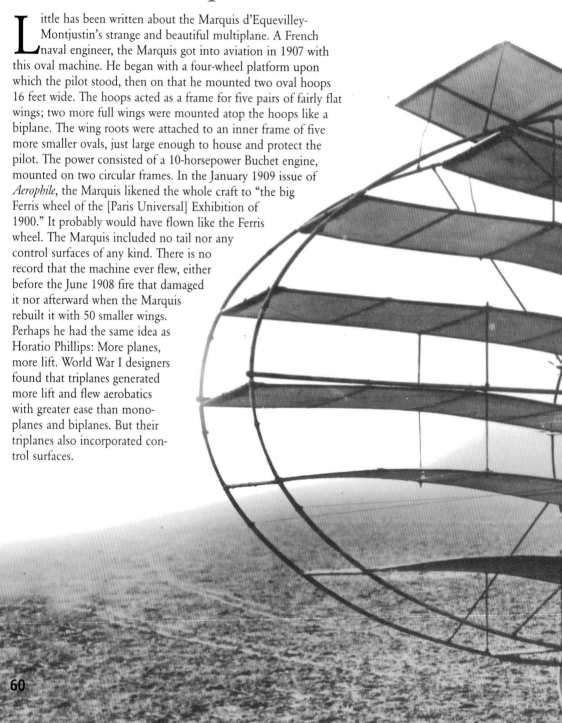

Little has been written about the Marquis d'Equevilley-Montjustin's strange and beautiful multiplane. A French naval engineer, the Marquis got into aviation in 1907 with this oval machine. He began with a four-wheel platform upon which the pilot stood, then on that he mounted two oval hoops 16 feet wide. The hoops acted as a frame for five pairs of fairly flat wings; two more full wings were mounted atop the hoops like a biplane. The wing roots were attached to an inner frame of five more smaller ovals, just large enough to house and protect the pilot. The power consisted of a 10-horsepower Buchet engine, mounted on two circular frames. In the January 1909 issue of *Aerophile*, the Marquis likened the whole craft to "the big Ferris wheel of the [Paris Universal] Exhibition of 1900." It probably would have flown like the Ferris wheel. The Marquis included no tail nor any control surfaces of any kind. There is no record that the machine ever flew, either before the June 1908 fire that damaged it nor afterward when the Marquis rebuilt it with 50 smaller wings. Perhaps he had the same idea as Horatio Phillips: More planes, more lift. World War I designers found that triplanes generated more lift and flew aerobatics with greater ease than mono-planes and biplanes. But their triplanes also incorporated con-trol surfaces.

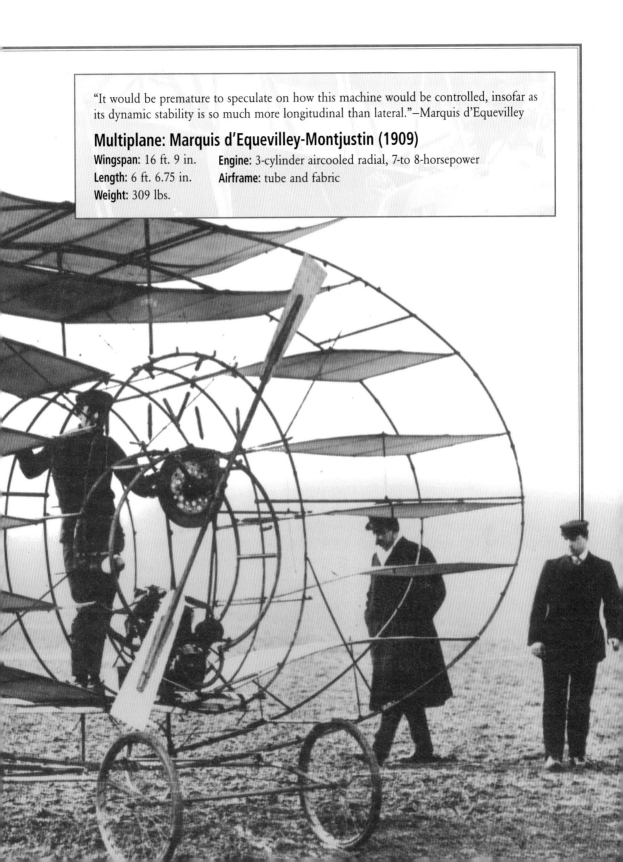

"It would be premature to speculate on how this machine would be controlled, insofar as its dynamic stability is so much more longitudinal than lateral."–Marquis d'Equevilley

Multiplane: Marquis d'Equevilley-Montjustin (1909)

Wingspan: 16 ft. 9 in. **Engine:** 3-cylinder aircooled radial, 7-to 8-horsepower
Length: 6 ft. 6.75 in. **Airframe:** tube and fabric
Weight: 309 lbs.

One quarter rear right side view of Equevilley Multiplane (1909), designed by the Marquis d'Equevilley-Montjustin, on the ground, probably at Issy-les-Moulineaux, Paris, France.

GIVAUDAN

Flying Tubes

Another tractor aircraft came along in 1909. Designed by a Frenchman named Givaudan, it had two...well...wings, one on either end of the flying machine. Actually these wings were circular, or annular as the aeronautical engineers call them, although they had no curved surface to provide lift. The wings were attached together by a fuselage consisting of little more than metal tubing, and the pilot sat directly behind the engine that drove that tractor prop. Its control system amounted to nothing, really: the front wing could be swiveled in any direction thanks to a U-joint. It rested on four bicycle wheels–two on the bottom of the back wing and two on the forward fuselage. Despite arousing great interest among aviation circles it never got off the ground. It did, however, pave the way for circular airfoils that emerged in the late 1940s.

Givaudan (1909)

Wingspan: Annular, divided by eight radial planes

Length: 19 ft.

Engine: Vermorel 8-cylinder air-cooled inline V, 40-horsepower

Airframe: metal tubing and wood, with fabric covering

COANDA TURBO-PROPULSEUR

Prehistoric Jet

One of the first things you'd notice about this slim biplane was its lack of propeller. Designed by 24-year-old Romanian Henri Coanda, the airplane made its official debut at the October 1910 *Salon de l'Aeronatique* in Paris, where it wowed the crowd. That's not only because the biplane had a complete wooden cover, and its struts and bracing wires were kept to a bare minimum, but also because its tractor-mounted engine drove a centrifugal compressor through a series of gears. And that meant it was the very first jet airplane. But while it looked nice just sitting there at the Salon, it did not have the right stuff to lift off the ground. The Coanda weighed 926 pounds, yet its 50-horsepower engine only produced 450 pounds of thrust. Henri Coanda moved to Britain in 1912 and had a fine career as a designer at the Bristol aircraft company. In the 1930s, however, two designers—Britain's Frank Whittle and Germany's Hans von Ohain—took a page from Coanda's book and designed the world's first true jet engines.

HENRI COANDA

Coanda Turbo-propulseur

Wingspan: 33 ft. 1.5 in.

Length: 39 ft. 7.25 in.

Weight: 926 lbs.

Height: 9 ft. .25 in.

Engine: Clerget 4-cylinder water-cooled inline driving centrifugal air compressor generating 50-horsepower

Airframe: Plywood-covered steel tubing

Left side view of central section of Coanda 1910 Turbo-Propulseur Sesquiplane on exhibit (Exhibit No. 187) at the 2e Exposition Internationale de Locomotion Aérienne (2nd Salon de l'Aviation), held in the Grand Palais, Paris, France from October 15 to November 2, 1910.

SIKORSKY H-2 HELICOPTER [1910]

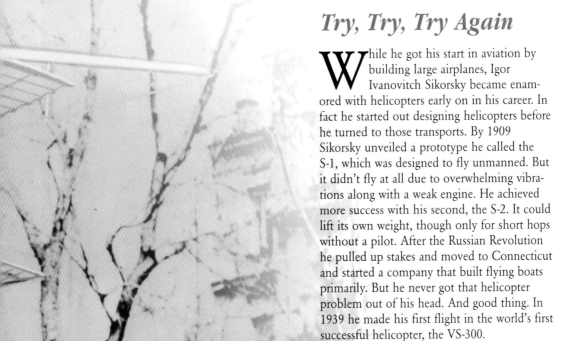

Try, Try, Try Again

While he got his start in aviation by building large airplanes, Igor Ivanovitch Sikorsky became enamored with helicopters early on in his career. In fact he started out designing helicopters before he turned to those transports. By 1909 Sikorsky unveiled a prototype he called the S-1, which was designed to fly unmanned. But it didn't fly at all due to overwhelming vibrations along with a weak engine. He achieved more success with his second, the S-2. It could lift its own weight, though only for short hops without a pilot. After the Russian Revolution he pulled up stakes and moved to Connecticut and started a company that built flying boats primarily. But he never got that helicopter problem out of his head. And good thing. In 1939 he made his first flight in the world's first successful helicopter, the VS-300.

1912 AVIETTE

Downhill Bicyclist

English artist Jose Weiss caught the flying bug in the first decade of the 20th century, and he designed a few flying machines beginning around 1909. Perhaps his most famous was the Aviette, built in 1912. It had no tail, and Weiss expected to bicycle it into the air. There exist three types of Aviette photos: Those of it resting on the ground, those of it taking off from a hill, and those of it crashing soon after.

Head-on view of Larribe 1912
Aviette at an unknown event,
probably somewhere in France.

70

FABRÉ HYDRAVION

Pushed off From the Water With a Giant Spray...

In 1909 Wilbur Wright flew one of his aeroplanes from New York's Governor's Island and up the river during that year's Hudson-Fulton Celebration. Since he was flying over water he was careful to attach a canoe to the bottom of his flying machine. But because it didn't take off or land in the water the machine could not be called the first floatplane. That honor belongs to Henri Fabré, who in 1910 lifted off from a harbor near Marseilles in his Hydravion. The aircraft was a pusher canard monoplane that rested on three flat-bottom, skid-like floats, while the pilot sat atop the connecting framework. On March 28, 1910 the first-time flier Fabré skimmed along the water, reached an altitude of just over six feet, and flew along for about a mile and a quarter, then landed—the first person in history to do such a thing.

HENRI FABRÉ

Fabré Hydravion

Wingspan: 45 ft. 11 in.
Length: 27 ft. 10.5 in.
Weight: 1,047 lbs.
Height: 12 ft. 1.75 in.
Engine: Gnome aircooled
7-cylinder rotary,
50-horsepower

THE PFITZNER 1910 MONOPLANE

Just Helping the Boss

More just a little bad blood flowed between the Wright brothers and Glenn Curtiss. The Wrights invented what they called wingwarping, a technique for twisting the wingtips in opposite directions manipulated by the pilot to lift one side or the other so that the plane would fly level and could make banked turns. It was the final piece of the aeronautical puzzle that allowed the airplane to be controlled in the air. They patented it, and within a couple of years Glenn Curtiss infringed on that patent. He tried everything to show the courts that someone else had thought of or could have thought of something like wingwarping, or ailerons as the more evolved system later became known. Enter Alexander Pfitzner, who was superintendent of the Curtiss engine department. In early 1910 he built a monoplane with what he called "equalizers" inserted into each end of the wing. When an equalizer was

deployed its drag slowed the machine and it turned, and the same drag lowered the wing if it was high. In short, it performed exactly the same task as the Wrights' wingwarping. Interesting that Pfitzner worked for Curtiss. Anyway, the monoplane incorporated some other unusual features. The pusher airplane sat on four wheels, and its rudder and elevator were both positioned in front of the pilot's seat. These controls were wired to the control column, while today's airplanes use rudder pedals. Its first flight was in February, and

Pfitzner took off and slammed into a tree. More often than not his flights ended badly, but on April 5, 1910 he made 13 successful flights in his machine. Soon after Pfitzner left Curtiss for the Burgess Co., and he brought along his dark monoplane. The company bought it and then sold it for $4000. That very same year, on July 12, 1910, Pfitzner committed suicide. As it turned out his control system was slightly ahead of its time: after World War II the Aircoupe came out with rudders that the pilot controlled through the steering wheel instead of pedals.

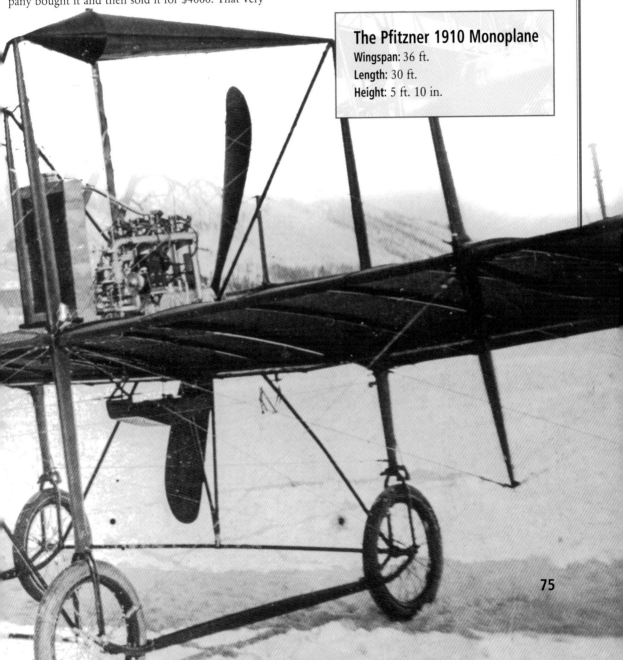

The Pfitzner 1910 Monoplane
Wingspan: 36 ft.
Length: 30 ft.
Height: 5 ft. 10 in.

Left rear view of the Pfitzner Monoplane wrecked on the ice at Lake Keuka, Hammondsport, New York, winter of 1909-1910

VIN FIZ FLYER

Not Much Made it to the Finish Line

Back around 1911 one William Randolph Hearst put up $50,000 for the first person to fly across the United States in 30 days or less. Cal Rogers declared he'd try it, and got a fizzy grape drink company to sponsor the trip. He named his airplane the Vin Fiz Flyer, after the fizzy grape drink. The flying machine was a Wright Model EX, which, of all the Wright brothers' machines, resembled an airplane the most. Sure, the pilot sat out in the open, it had that single engine that drove two pusher props with bicycle chains, and it had that two lever system (one lever that controlled the rudder and another that controlled the wingwarping), and it positively dripped with the Vin Fiz logo. But its rudder and elevators were in back and that counted for something–at least for the Wright brothers. On September 17, 1911 Rogers left from Sheepshead Bay, Brooklyn and followed the Iron Compass (the railroad) west by southwest. On his first of 69 landings he crashed. He would go on to crash an additional 15 times. Once his engine exploded, shooting hot shrapnel into his flesh. He had the metal pulled out and a new engine installed. By the time he reached Pasadena, California, on November 5, 1911, the only original parts that made it all the way from

Sheepshead bay were two wing struts and the rudder. The airplane had been destroyed five times. The last leg of the flight he flew with crutches and a broken ankle. With an average speed of 52 miles per hour, it had taken him 49 days. That was 19 days longer than Hearst had stipulated, but Vin Fiz did pay him $5 for each mile–4,321 miles–that he flew. He ended up with $21,605, but didn't have much time to spend it. On April 3, 1912 he crashed into a Pacific beach and died, trapped beneath the wreckage.

CALBRAITH P. ROGERS

Rogers, in Chicago, had only two days to go on the cross-country contest. A reporter asked if Cal would continue. "I am bound for Los Angeles and the Pacific ocean," Rogers said. "Prize or no prize, that's where I am bound and if canvas, steel and wire together with a little brawn, tendon, and brain stick with me, I mean to get there… I'm going to do this whether I get five thousand dollars or fifty cents or nothing. I am going to cross this continent simply to be the first to cross in an aeroplane."

Vin Fiz Flyer (1911)

Wingspan: 32 ft. **Length:** 28 ft. (approx.)
Max Weight: 1,250 lbs. (approx.)
Engine: Wright 6-cylinder air-cooled
Airframe: canvas-covered wood

One of the many crashes…

PETRÓCZY-KÁRMÁN-ZUROVEC PKZ-2 HELICOPTER

Some Things a Balloon Did Better

During World War I armies used tethered observation balloons to check on enemy movements in the trenches. Being eyes in the sky these volatile hydrogen balloons were the target of fighter aircraft firing incendiary bullets and, simply put, there was no way to reel them down fast enough once the fighter got them in their sites. In 1916 the Austrian Army Balloon Corps came up with a substitute. This was the first helicopter to achieve sustained–though tethered–flight. Invented by Wilhelm Zurovec, with this helicopter designed by Austria's Lt. Stephan Petróczy von Petróczy with input from famed Theodore von Kármán, the machine had three 120-horsepower rotary engines driving two 19-feet 8-inches counter-rotating propellers, upon which sat the observer's round basket -

that's right, he sat *above* the propellers. Meant solely for vertical lift, the machine required three cables attached from a lower tubular framework to the ground in an attempt to keep the helicopter stable. To raise and lower it the crew used a single cable attached to the machine's center. Unlike an observation balloon the observer had no parachute from which to escape the machine. Instead the whole machine had a parachute. Without any directional control the helicopter flew precariously. While the military was more comfortable with observation balloons, the captive helicopter was a step toward developing rotary-wing aircraft that would eventually fly without the restraint of tethers.

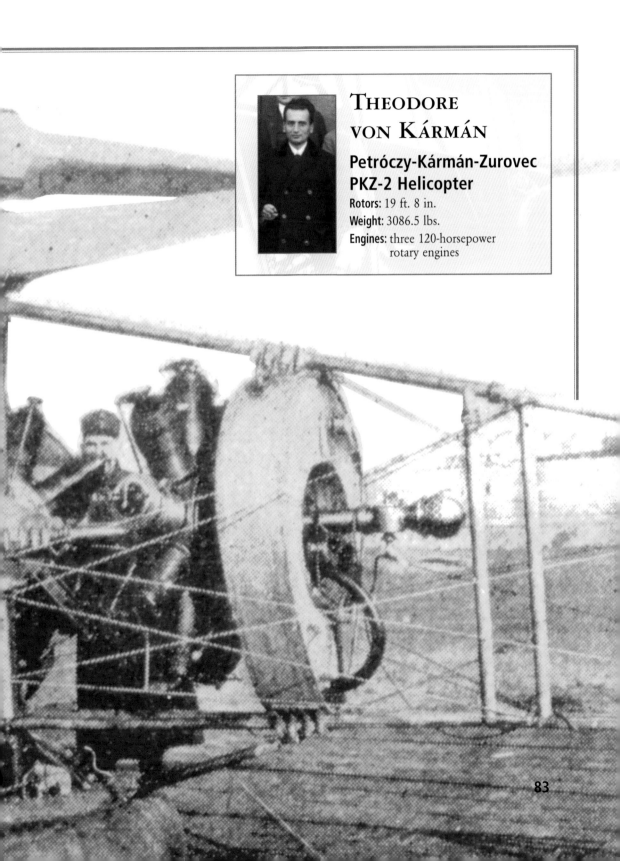

THEODORE VON KÁRMÁN

Petróczy-Kármán-Zurovec PKZ-2 Helicopter

Rotors: 19 ft. 8 in.

Weight: 3086.5 lbs.

Engines: three 120-horsepower rotary engines

CURTISS AUTOPLANE

A Little Wide for the Road

The Autoplane, a 1917 hybrid AKA Curtiss Model 11, first appeared at New York City's Pan-American Aeronautic Exposition. Unlike its subsequent aerocars, the Autoplane had 40-foot long fixed triplane wings (which arrived straight from the Curtiss Model L) permanently attached to a special four-wheel, aluminum, three-seat body. The pilot sat in front, while two passengers sat side-by-side just behind him. The engine, a Curtiss OXX generating 100-horsepower, was placed in the nose, and through a shaft and gearbox it not only drove the rear two wheels but also the pusher prop. The pusher was made possible by twin tails and lots of wire bracing; the machine also had a forward canard. As a car it sped along at up to 65 miles per hour; as an airplane it flew once but rather poorly. The company abandoned the concept in no time at all, while airplane-car hybrids have tended to rear their ugly tails at ever increasing intervals since.

Curtiss Autoplane [1917]
Wingspan: 40 ft. 4 in.
Engine: 100-horsepower Curtiss OXX
Top Speed: 65 m.p.h. (as an airplane)

87

Rear view of the Curtiss Autoplane

FOKKER DR.1

Small, Slow, and Highly Maneuverable

Anthony Fokker built the Fokker Dr.1 triplane in 1917. Its wings were shorter than most other contemporary fighters, and they produced more drag, which slowed the airplane a bit. But on the bright side those three short wings made it perhaps the most maneuverable fighter of the war. The Dr. stood for Dridecker, which means triplane. Not only was it slower, the Dr.1 was also small for a fighter. Yet Von Richtofen, the Red Baron, loved his. But after Canadian Roy Brown in his Sopwith Camel—or Australian troops on the ground—shot down Von Richtofen on April 21, 1918, the triplane fell from grace.

The Red Baron, Manfred Von Richtofen

FOK
2251

985

ANTHONY FOKKER

Fokker Dr.1
Wingspan: 23 ft. 7.5 in.
Length: 18 ft. 11 in.
Height: 9 ft. 8 in.
Weight: 1,289 lbs.
Max. Speed: 103 m.p.h.
Engine: One 110-horsepower, 9-cylinder Le Rhone rotary

TARRANT TABOR

The Tarrants of Spring

The 1919 Tarrant Tabor was one huge airplane. Actually a triplane with more braces than a rich kid with crooked teeth, the craft's center wing measured 131 feet 3 in. Its entire wing area measured almost 5,000 square feet and the whole airplane weighed a whopping 44,672 pounds. Built by the British as a bomber for the Great War, the Tabor just barely missed participating. Its power came from six Napier Lions, each generating 450-horsepower. The builders placed four, tractor-style, atop the lower two wings, while they mounted two pushers on the bottom wing. Its very first takeoff, in May 1919, began

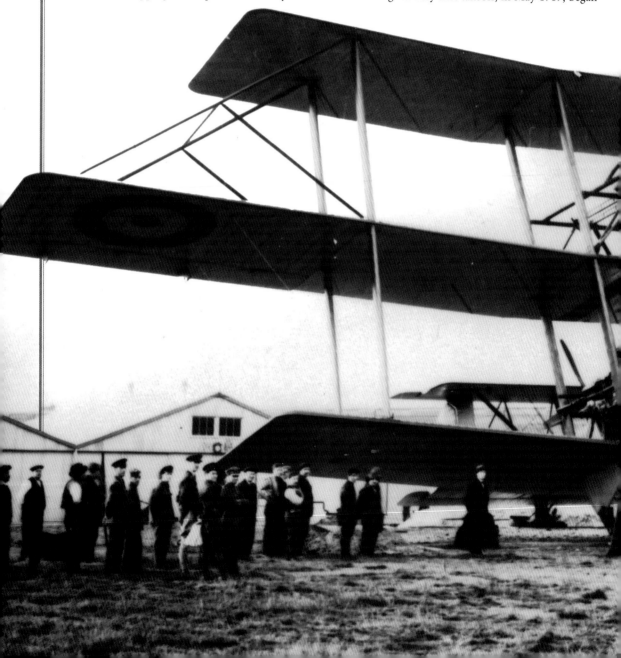

with the test pilot using mainly the four bottom engines. Then he applied power to the top two engines and the substantial distance from those engines to the ground was more than the elevators could handle. The aircraft nosed over, killing the pilot. The project was canceled.

Tarrant Tabor [1919]

Wingspan: 131 ft. 3 in. (center wing)
Max. Weight: 44,672 lbs.
Engines: six 450-horsepower Napier Lions

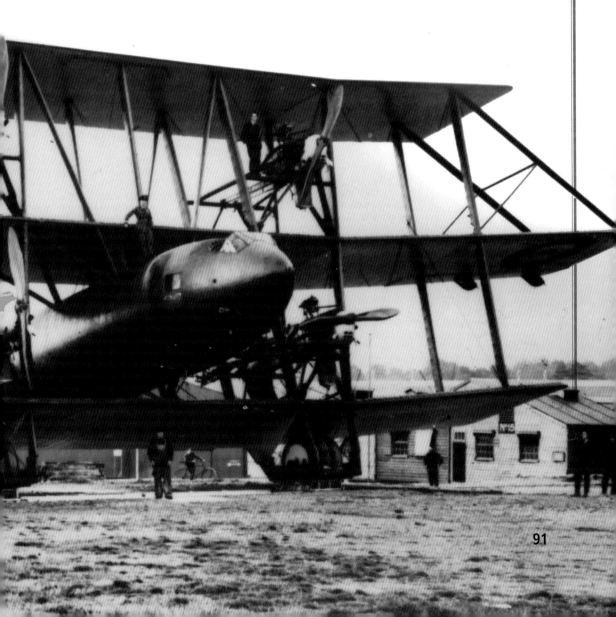

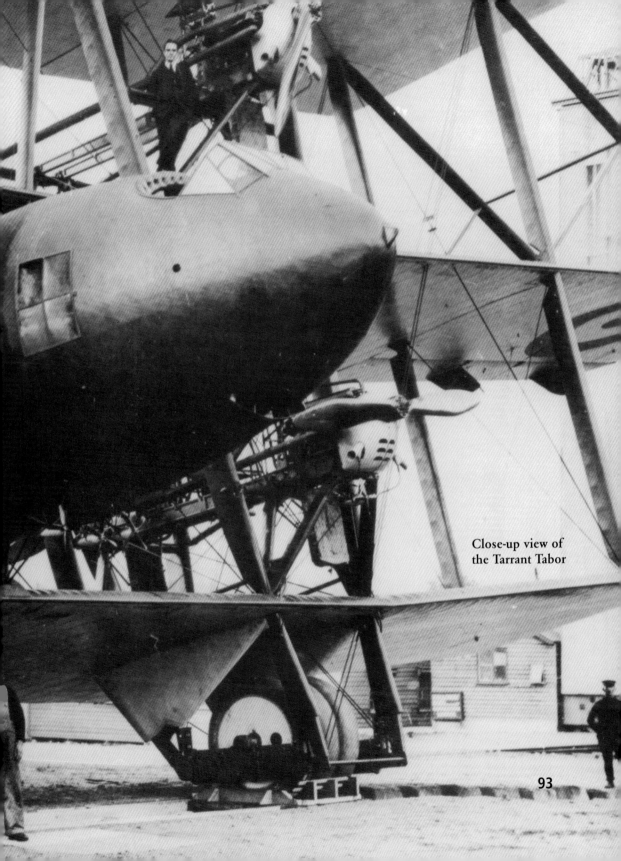

Close-up view of
the Tarrant Tabor

Caproni Ca.60

Damaged Beyond Care

The 1921 Italian Ca.60 Transaero really looked like less of an airplane and more like a comfy houseboat. Its fuselage was long and square, and had plenty of windows. For its proposed flights, across the Atlantic, 100 passengers could fit comfortably in the hull. Evenly spaced above the houseboat were three sets of tandem triplane wings, all nine the same length, all nine with a set of ailerons. The last wings housed the rudder and elevators. The total wing area was a whopping 9,000 feet, making it the largest airplane in its day. The lowest center wing had large lifeboat-size sponsons on either end to prevent it from rolling over. It sported eight engines: three tractor engines in the front, three pusher engines in the rear, and a pusher and a tractor on the opposite side of the center engines fore and aft. They were all Liberty engines, which were only exceded in inept function by the Curtiss OX-5 series. It flew exactly once: from Lake Maggiore. After reaching an altitude of 60 feet the flying houseboat took a nosedive and broke up when it hit the water. After it sank, the company had no more Ca.60s left.

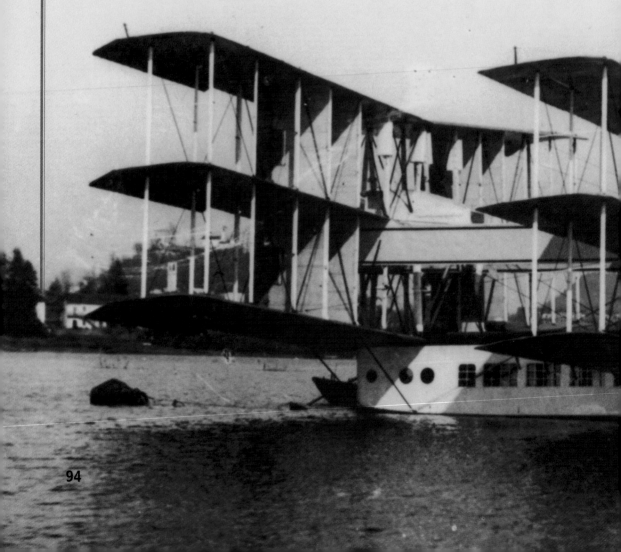

94

GIANNI CAPRONI

Ca.60 Transaero

Wingspan: 100 ft.
Max Weight: 55,000 lbs.
Engine: eight 400-horsepower Liberty engines
Est. Top Speed: 90 m.p.h.

BURNELLI LIFTING BODIES

Flying Airfoil

Aviation historians have argued the viability of Vincent Burnelli's concept for more than a half-century. Burnelli thought the fuselage itself should be airfoil shape–like the wings–to provide additional lift. Make the fuselage wide enough and you could pack in more cargo, more people, more everything. And that airfoil shape would make it more solid and crashworthy. So in 1922 he built the RB-2, a large biplane with its twin engines mounted within the tip of the airfoil fuselage. Over the years he kept refining the design, building airfoil fuselages with single wings, twin booms, and on and on. Each time he'd get more backers and more

money, Burnelli would build another airfoil fuselage with wings. Legend has it that a spat with Franklin D. Roosevelt on the eve of World War II prevented Burnelli from receiving a lucrative government contract. In truth his machines didn't fly as fast as their contemporaries, and in fact every fuselage is a streamline lifting body. And whether square, round or rectangular, a fuselage can only do so much to protect the passengers and pilots. In more recent years, however, NASA has experimented with lifting bodies such as the X-33 spaceplane and the X-43 hypersonic scramjet. The space agency canceled the former in 2001 and is still experimenting with the latter's viability.

Vincent Burnelli

In 1964 a group called the Long Island Early Flyers elected to present Vincent Burnelli with the Billy Mitchell medal. The ceremony was to take place on Sunday, June 21st, 1964, but Burnelli suffered a fatal heart attack just two days before and never received his award.

Burnelli RB-2

Wingspan: 80 ft.   **Length:** 46 ft.

Max. Weight: up to 9 tons

Engine: two 650-horsepower Galloway Atlantics; changed to 600-horsepower Rolls-Royce Condors

97

PESCARA'S HELICOPTER

Rotor-Rama

By all accounts it was the very first helicopter to hover above the ground for one minute, and it occurred at a Paris airfield back in 1922. Spaniard Marquis Pateras de Pescara had built a two rotor machine—each consisting of six biplane wings braced with the usual struts and wires. The wings rotating in opposite directions to eliminate torque and provide stability. The Marquis also invented a system that could change the blades' pitch while the machine was flying. The whole thing was driven by one 170-horsepower Hispano-Suiza powerplant, but if it should die the wings would continue turning as

the helicopter dropped due to the airflow from the descent. On the ground it rested on four wheels. Two years later Pescara's built his third helicopter, No. 3, outfitted with a 180-horsepower Hispano motor, and managed a 10-minute flight. Previously, in 1907, the Breguet brothers, Louis and Jacques, built a four-biplane-rotored machine, each held on to the end of a horizontal steel cross where the pilot sat. Driven by a 50-horsepower Antoinette, their Gyroplane No. 1 lifted two feet off the ground—with four men holding the machine steady.

MARQUIS PATERAS DE PESCARA

As a result of his helicopter work Pescara received a number of patents–including one covering autorotation (that is, flying a helicopter without an engine), and for a cyclic pitch control that changes the rotors pitch and allows the helicopter to lift and land vertically and fly horizontally.

GERHARDT CYCLEPLANE

Pedal till the Wings Fall off

This looked like just about any other airplane of the early 1920s except it had seven wings. And then there was Gerhardt's method of propulsion: bicycle power. Since high-aspect ratio wings were the best way to get into the air with lower, bicycle speed drag, the wingspan would need to be longer than a battleship to get the Cycleplane airborne. So Gerhardt divided that wing and came up with seven. Of course he had to add the drag of all those struts and wires from all those wings. But he forgot all about that. It didn't matter anyway. Built lightly, the Cycleplane's top wings collapsed on its only take-off run. It wasn't until the 1970s with aeronautical engineer Paul MacCreedy's Gossamer Condor, Gossamer Albatross, and Daedalus, that the bicycle-driven airplane flew successfully.

Left side view of Gerhardt Cycleplane

Gerhardt Cycleplane
Wings: 9
Engine: human legs

MAIWURM TILT WING

Over a Barrel

Mission Beach, California, resident Paul Maiwurm got the idea to build a tilt-wing aircraft in 1929. But it wasn't just any tilt-wing: It had this rotating barrel that Maiwurm thought would create what he called a "cyclonic vortex." He designed his machine's barrel and top wing to tilt upward during takeoff, and then tilt down for level flight. For controls the machine had farings that the pilot could move together or one at a time, and so they acted not only as ailerons but also as elevators and flaps. On its test flight–which Maiwurm wasn't shy about publicizing–the tilt-wing began vibrating, and then suffered a complete collapse. It never even got into the air. The inventor, who optimistically applied for and received a patent on the machine, shoved what was left into Mission Bay.

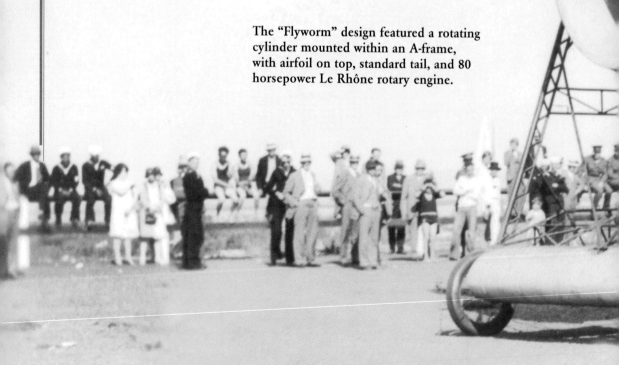

The "Flyworm" design featured a rotating cylinder mounted within an A-frame, with airfoil on top, standard tail, and 80 horsepower Le Rhône rotary engine.

Maiwurm Tilt Wing
Engine: 80 horsepower LeRhône rotary

Left rear view of Maiwurm's 1929 "Flyworm" Flying Machine on the ground at its first public ground test at Mission Beach, San Diego, California, June 23, 1929.

BLÉRIOT 125

Art Deco Airplane

Depending on your definition of high-wing or low-wing, the 1930 Blériot monoplane was both. It had a high wing for the twin booms that each held six passengers in luxury; they could peer through the large forward windows and see where the airplane was going. Each boom, by the way, had baggage compartments and a toilet; and each boom was connected at the tail with a monoplane tailplane. To the three-man crew, however, the aircraft was a low-wing, since they rode in a center boom above the other passenger booms. On either end of the central boom a Hispano-Suiza engine was mounted in tractor-pusher fashion. The aircraft was exhibited at the 1930 Paris *Salon de l'Aeronautique*. But when it underwent flight tests in March 1931 the results weren't so great; it displayed very poor qualities in flight. Testing continued until 1933, but the aircraft succeeded to fail to gain its flight certification. Blériot personnel scrapped the 125 the next year.

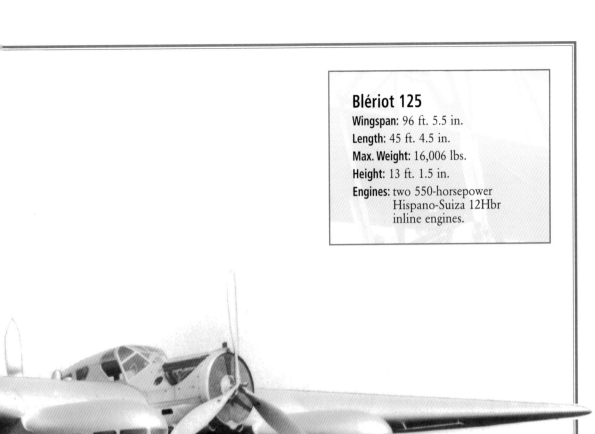

Blériot 125

Wingspan: 96 ft. 5.5 in.

Length: 45 ft. 4.5 in.

Max. Weight: 16,006 lbs.

Height: 13 ft. 1.5 in.

Engines: two 550-horsepower Hispano-Suiza 12Hbr inline engines.

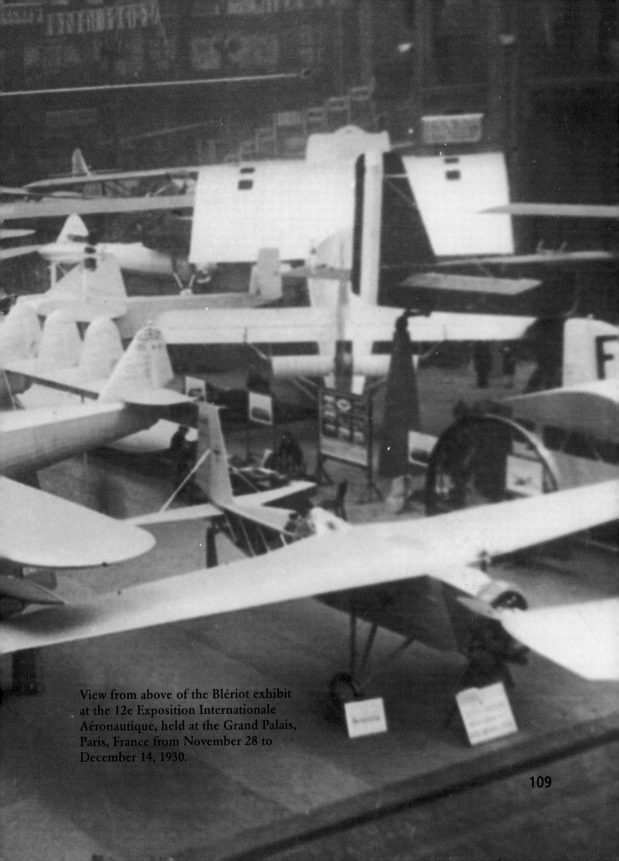

View from above of the Blériot exhibit at the 12e Exposition Internationale Aéronautique, held at the Grand Palais, Paris, France from November 28 to December 14, 1930.

FLORINE TANDEM ROTOR HELICOPTER

Two Rotor Heads are Better than One

In 1929 Nicolas Florine, an engineer born in Russia and a resident of Belgium, designed and built a tandem-rotor helicopter. He took a different path from the other helicopter afficionados of the day: while the rotors on his machine revolved in the same direction, he had them tilt in opposite directions to cancel the torque. His first helicopter didn't see the end of 1930. But his next one flew well. In 1933 it flew more than nine minutes and reached a nose-bleed altitude of 15 feet. But, discouraged by the complexities of rotary-wing flight, Florine quit working on them in the days before World War II–a war that ended up destroying his helicopters.

GEE BEE R-1 SUPER SPORTSTER

An Airplane Built Around an Engine

The five Granville brothers got into building racing airplanes during the genre's heyday in the 1930s. Zantford, after all, was an auto mechanic who got his pilot's license in the late 1920s and he talked his brothers into moving to an airport outside of Boston to work on airplanes. Pretty soon they formed Gee Bee and were manufacturing their own. The first one, designed by Howell Miller, was also his most unusual design, even for the early 1930s. Called the R-1 Super Sportster (the sister ship was the R-2), it was a stubby affair, built entirely around its powerful 1,334 cubic inch, 800-horsepower, 9-cylinder Pratt & Whitney Wasp Sr. Radial. In other words, the R-1 was all engine. The red-and-white fuselage was but 17 feet 9 inches long, and its cockpit was positioned way back and flowed into the vertical stabilizer. The wing measured 25 feet long and had a chord of 53 inches at the root. And it would fly fast: top speed reached 300 miles per hour. But of the three or so pilots who flew it in the air races only one survived: Jimmy Doolittle. The rest crashed and died in the wreckage. According to Delmar Benjamin, who has been flying his replica Gee Bee R-1 on the airshow circuit for more than a decade now, the reason for their crashes was simple: No pilot was used to flying such a high-powered, high-torque machine before the war.

After World War II such pilots became commonplace, having trained on fighters such as the P-47

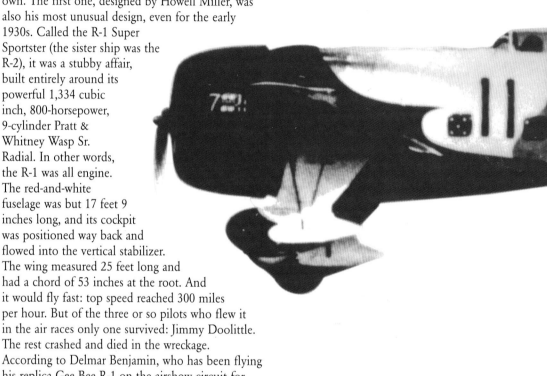

Thunderbolt and the P-51 Mustang. Zantford died in a crash of one the last Gee Bee Sportsters that he was flying to a customer in South Carolina. Upon seeing a construction crew on the airstrip, he tried to abort landing by quickly pulling up. In doing that, the engine failed and he crashed. In 1934 the Gee Bee company filed for bankruptcy.

Jimmy Doolittle

Gee Bee R-1 Super Sportster
Wingspan: 25 ft.
Length: 17 ft. 9 in.
Gross Weight: 3,075 lbs.
Engine: One Pratt & Whitney Wasp Sr., 1,334-cubic inch 9-cylinder radial developing 800-horsepower
Speed: 300 m.p.h.

HERRICK VERTOPLANE

An Autogyro With Real Wings

The typical autogyro doesn't have a powered rotor; it spins as the engine and tractor prop start the aircraft rolling, then the airstream keeps the rotor rotating. An autogyro can take off and land in a few feet–less than an airplane, but more than a helicopter. And autogyros can't hover. Both the helicopter and the autogyro, however, are slower than their fixed wing counterparts. Anyway, in 1931 a man named Gerald Herrick got this great idea on how to speed up the autogyro. His HV-1 Vertoplane was a single-blade autogyro that could take off and land in a few feet as the upper blade turned, then the pilot would fix the symmetrical blade perpendicular to the fuselage and parallel to the full-length bottom wing. That turned the whole machine into a biplane–and fly as fast as one, too. Herrick first tested the concept in a wind tunnel, then test-flew the machine as a biplane from a runway. It worked fine. Next he tried to convert it from a biplane to an autogyro in flight, but the HV-1 would have none of that: It crashed.

Herrick wasn't deterred. In 1937 he built the HV-2, shortened the top wing, and changed the name to Vertaplane. This version could change from biplane to autogyro, but it had a slew of other problems that Herrick found difficult to overcome. The advent of World War II–and the 1939 Sikorsky helicopter–finished off the autogyro for good.

Herrick HV-2A Vertaplane

GERALD HERRICK

Gerard Herrick was a cousin of Myron T. Herrick–the American ambassador who was there to meet Charles Lindbergh when he landed at Le Borget in Paris.

One-half left rear view of the Herrick HV-1
Vertaplane on the ground.

Four Wings, No Waiting

Like the name implies, Supermarine designed the World War I "Nighthawk" twin-engine, four-wing airplane for night patrols. It carried two Lewis guns, one in the nose and one in the tail. It also came equipped with a two-pound Davis gun mounted on its top wing, which could fire in any direction thanks to a double parallel sliding bed. This was one well-thought-out machine. It had a gimbal-mounted searchlight, a wireless telegraph, and no fewer than nine fuel tanks. If one should be struck by enemy fire it could be shut down from the cockpit.

That is provided it didn't burst into flames. All the engine and control lines were covered in armor and placed outside the fuselage. And since this machine was to fly long patrols at night there was a bunk where one airman could rest or sleep. There was one small problem with it, however: it was underpowered. After modifications to the props the military decided the Nighthawk should fly off into the sunset. Yet during World War II nearly all combatant nations fielded night fighters, albeit ones equipped with radar to spot enemy aircraft in the dark skies.

XF-11

The Airplane that Put Hughes into a Downward Spiral

Howard Hughes's XF-11 had the same layout as Lockheed's P-38 Lightning, though the former used radial engines instead of the latter's two inlines. The XF-11 was bigger, too, and at the time the heaviest twin-engine airplane in the world. Hughes designed it as a high-speed photo reconnaissance machine especially for the 1946 invasion of Japan, although it might have made a good night fighter. The Army Air Force even ordered 98 XF-11s. Its test pilots said it performed well, especially in stalls. But fate played a hand. On July 7, 1946, Hughes took the airplane up for its first flight, then one of its propellers suddenly went into reverse pitch. He lost control and took off

470156

120

the roof of a house before crashing. A Marine sergeant pulled the badly injured millionaire from the wreckage, and through sheer will Hughes recovered. There was a second XF-11 which test pilots wrung out over several years, but eventually the Air Force decided to invest its reconnaissance budget in jets. In the end they scrapped the only surviving XF-11.

"...massive and mean..."
–Hughes factory ground crews

XF-11

Wingspan: 101 ft. 5 in.
Length: 65 ft. 5 in.
Height: 23 ft. 3 in.
Maximum weight: 58,678 lbs.
Maximum Speed: 449 m.p.h.
Range: 5,000 miles
Engines: Two 3,000-horsepower Pratt & Whitney R-4360 Wasp major radials

THE BUDD CONESTOGA

Stainless Steel Never Needs Polishing

In the early 1940s Edward Budd Manufacturing Company of Philadelphia entered the Navy's competition for a twin-engine cargo carrier and troop transport. But the Budd Company also came up with new twist: Their Budd RB-1 Conestoga would be constructed entirely not of aluminum but shotwelded stainless steel. The US Navy liked the concept, and placed an order for 200 Conestogas in August 1942. Not to be outdone the Air Force, which called it the C-93, placed an order for 600. The Conestoga was a high-wing cantilever monoplane with tricycle gear, not unlike the later (all-aluminum) C-123 but with a large nose the shape of

W. C. Fields's. Though theoretically safer than an aluminum airplane in a crash, the Conestoga had its share of construction problems: an all-steel aircraft is easier to say than to build. And costs rose logarithmically. By 1944 the Army had all but won the war, so it canceled its contract. The Navy sliced its contract from 200 down to 25, which were then sold off to the highest bidder. As far as is known, there are no Conestogas left, save wood and canvas ones in pioneer museums. Even though the plane did not last, the concept of welding took off when engineers adopted the idea of eliminating drag-inducing rivets.

Budd RB-1 Conestoga

Wingspan: 100 ft.
Length: 68 ft.
Max. Weight: 33,860 lbs.
Height: 31 ft. 9 in.

Engines: two 1,200 Pratt & Whitney -1830 Twin Wasp radial engines.
Max Speed: 197 m.p.h.

Three-quarter right front view from slightly above of fuselage of Budd RB-1 Conestoga under static test assembly at the Edward G. Budd Mfg. Co., Philadelphia, Pennsylvania, July 9, 1943

CUSTER CHANNEL WING

Custer's Last, um, Flight?

It begs a joke, but the Channel Wing wasn't what you'd call Custer's Last Stand. It wasn't what you'd call a great idea however, unless you really, really wanted to shorten a prop plane's wing. Inventor William Custer came up with the concept and finished the prototype in 1942. Each wing had a section that dipped into a half circle, which housed a pusher engine. His idea was that the engine would suck the air through the wing instead of simply dragging the wing along. Why he didn't consider using a pusher engine to do the same thing we'll never know. His prototype did have a slower stall speed than its contemporaries, and flew just well enough to encourage Custer. It didn't have enough lateral control, however, since Custer mounted the ailerons on winglets perpendicular to the upside-down channels. Eventually he placed the ailerons across the channels, and was satisfied with the performance. For his Last Stand (you knew that was coming), Custer built the CCW-5, basically the fuselage of a Baumann Brigadier twin with the twin channels housing two 275-horsepower Continental pusher engines. This tricycle-gear airplane had wings that extended well beyond the channels—wings that were long enough to support the Brigadier without the channels. The first and only production version rolled off the line in 1964, but Custer couldn't find investors to fund more channel wings. And that was Custer's Little Big Horn.

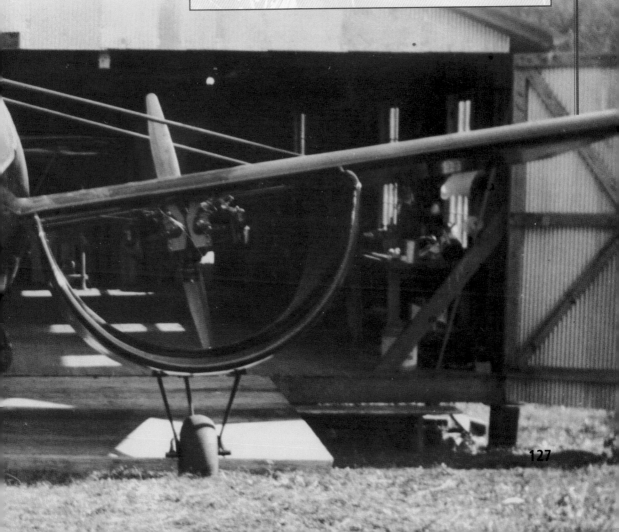

WILLIAM CUSTER

Willard R. Custer was indeed a relative of General George Custer. After his channel wing design failed to attract buyers Custer refused to give up his patents and the concept slipped into the pages of history. He died in 1985, but his son Harold has logged more than 1,000 hours in channel wings, and is working on an ultra light channel wing design of his own.

William R. Custer building channel spars
for the Custer Prototype in his
Hagerstown, Maryland, laboratory; 1948.

Look Ma! No Fuselage!

Northrop Aircraft, Inc. was formed in 1939; due to a special interest of President John Northrop (who designed the Lockheed Vega more than a decade before), the company built many a flying wing. The first, called the Northrop N-1M Jeep, was powered by two 65-horsepower pusher engines buried in the swept-back wing. Since engineers placed the cockpit on the wing, the pilot really couldn't see down. Nevertheless, the U.S. Army awarded Northrop a contract to build four experimental, tail-free, four-engine bombers, each of which could fly at some 200 miles per hour. Called the N-9M Flying Wing, the very first one flew in late December 1942, but after 50 test flights it crashed.

Testing continued on the other, and the final one reached a speed of 257 mph. Its contemporary, the Boeing B-17, had a greater top speed of 287 mph, and the later B-29 reached 358 mph. One more problem: even powered by jet engines the flying wing's speed limit hovered somewhere below supersonic. In the world of military pilots, speed is life. But eventually the flying wing research paid off. It turned out that the flying wing's radar return was the size of a small bird; in other words, it was one stealthy airplane. In the late 1980s Northrop unveiled its B-2 *Spirit* stealth bomber, a flying wing virtually invisible to enemy radar.

JOHN NORTHROP

Northrop N-1M

Wingspan: 38 ft.

Area: 300 sq. ft.

Max. Weight: 3,900 lbs

Engines: two 120-horsepower Franklin engines

Top Speed: 200 m.p.h.

Northrop N-9M Flying Wing under construction at the Northrop factory in California, April 3, 1944

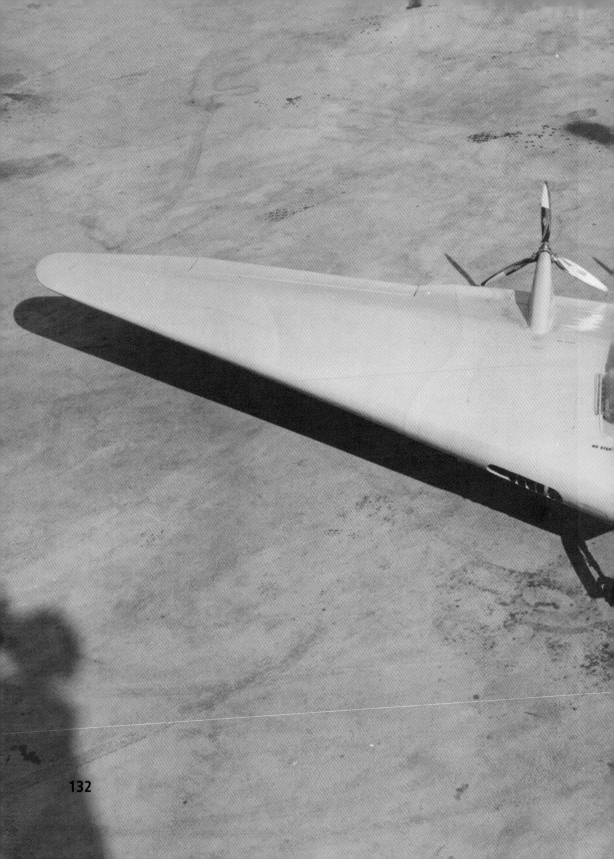

Top-front view of Northrop N-1M Jeep

Vought V-173 "Flying Pancake"

Flying Saucer—or Flapjack

Some people have seen flying saucers that presumably hold aliens from another planet. Social scientists think such sightings are due to increased paranoia that emerged from the Atomic Age and the Cold War. Others believe that those saucers are actually round-winged aircraft being tested by the US Air Force. One such aircraft: the World War II-era Vought V-173, perhaps better known as The "Flying Pancake". Unlike flying saucers the "Flying Pancake" could fly in only one direction: forward. First built by Chance-Vought Aircraft Company in 1942, the V-173 prototype had a pair of huge, slow propellers driven by two 80-horsepower Continental engine buried inside the wing. Unlike a "true" flying saucer, this airplane came equipped with twin rudders and combination aileron/elevators–elevons–mounted on the aft-mounted horizontal stabilizer.

The "Pancake" prototype's successful first flight, in late November 1942, led to more than 130 hours of test time in the air. It had a rather sluggish speed of 150 miles per hour, but it could also land at 35 mph–pretty good for aircraft carriers. So good, in fact, that the Navy signed a contract with Vought for a

prototype fighter, the XF5U-1. This little powerhouse was essentially a V-173 with retractable gear and twin Pratt & Whitney 1,350-horsepower mills. It had a slew of mechanical problems and Vought didn't complete it until 1948. By that time the Navy was all into jet fighters instead of piston-powered ones. So into jets, in fact, that they even refused to allow Vought to test the machine. And maybe the Navy was right. Its top speed, estimated at 390 mph, was much slower than contemporary piston fighters and up-and-coming jet warbirds. And so the "Flying Pancake" has disappeared— unless flying saucers really do exist.

Chance Vought V-173

Wingspan: 23 ft. 4 in.
Length: 26 ft. 8 in.
Empty Weight: 2,258 lbs.
Height: 12 ft. 11 in.
Engines: Two Continental A-80 engines of 80-horsepower each
Speed Range: 30 m.p.h. to 500 m.p.h.

Head-on view of Vought V-173 on the ground at unidentified airfield; circa mid- to late-1940s

137

HAFNER ROTABUGGY

A Jeep With Rotors

You could file this one under flying automobiles, except its wing was rotary. Built during World War II by the then-distressed British, the Rotabuggy was essentially a jeep or a truck with a rotor attached on the roof (it was detachable as well), and some sort of stabilizing fuselage in the back. Powered by one 90-horsepower engine, its maximum speed was 120 miles per hour. The concept was that it would be used for some sort of invasion, and the War Ministry tested it extensively in 1943 to 1944, but by the latter year more conventional weapons such as jeeps were wheeling right into the Third Reich. The idea was a good one, but it needed refinement. Starting with the Vietnam War, helicopters transported troops and ammunition to the battlefield and flew the wounded out. The Hafner Rotabuggy's day had yet to come.

Raoul Hafner

Raoul Hafner hailed from Austria, where in the 1920s he began working on designing rotorcraft of all kinds. In 1932 he abandoned Austria for England, and set up the Hafner Gyroplane Company. There, at Heston, Middlesex he labored throughout the war designing gyrocraft of all kinds. He even developed the man-carrying Rotochute, which could be deployed from an aircraft in an emergency.

Hafner Rotabuggy

Rotor Diameter: 32 ft. 10 in.
Length: 17 ft. 10 in.
Max. Weight: 3,111 lbs.
Empty Weight: 2,125 lbs.
Engine: 90 horsepower Pobjoy Niagara 7-cylinder radial
Max Speed: 150 m.p.h.
Liftoff/Landing Speed: 36 m.p.h.

One-half left rear view of Royal Air Force Hafner Rotabuggy experimental aircraft on the ground, probably preparatory to being towed into flight by the Armstrong Whitworth A.W. 38 Whitley bomber in background.

FIESELER FI 103R REICHENBER

If you Could only Get out in Time

The German V-1 was one of the first cruise missiles, and Hitler sent quite a few of these to terrorize London late in World War II. A couple of problems emerged, however: its control system was rather rudimentary, and alert British pilots could shoot them down. Also, the V-1 wasn't accurate against high-priority targets. The Fieseler company came up with a pretty good idea to counteract that: they built a V-1 with a pilot inside. The cockpit was in the fuselage, just below its pulse-jet engine. The concept was pretty simple: the pilot would aim the jet towards the target and just before impact, could bail out. Of course, that was made a bit difficult by the canopy's unreliable mechanism and the fact that the pilot would be jumping right in the jet's path. Luckily for the pilots, none were actually used against any targets. But as the Germans proved with the Me-262, the jet age had arrived.

A V-1 pulse-jet rocket photographed just after leaving the launch ramp

Fieseler Fi 103R Reichenberg
Wingspan: 18 ft. 9.25 in
Length: 26 ft. 3 in.
Engine: 772-lb-thrust Argus pulse-jet
Speed: 500 m.p.h.

V-1 flying bomb being transported on cart by German soldiers in preparation for launch across the English Channel

BLOHM UND VOSS BV 141

Room with a View

Back in the late 1930s when it appeared that the Nazis would rule the world, Germany decided it needed an observation plane that had great visiblity to scout out targets. Bv submitted the Blohm und Voss Bv 141, which had an asymmetrical layout: a tail boom with a radial engine on one side, and a shorter crew compartment (complete with camera) that was almost entirely windscreens on the other. There were three prototypes built in 1938, the last one armed with two 7.92 mm machine guns firing forward and two firing rearward. The manufacturer also added racks for four 110-pound bombs. The initial aircraft were considered underpowered, so an additional five Bv 141s were built with more powerful engines. Trials began in late 1941, and stopped in 1943 due to its low speed (compared with Allied fighters and bombers) and because the Luftwaffe needed more fighters to protect the Fatherland against around-the-clock Allied bombing.

Blohm und Voss Bv 141 [1941]

Span: 57 ft. 3.5 in.
Length: 45 ft. 9.25 in.
Height: 11 ft. 9.25 in.
Max weight: 12,566 lbs.
Engine: one 1,560-horsepower BMW 801A radial
Max speed: 230 m.p.h.

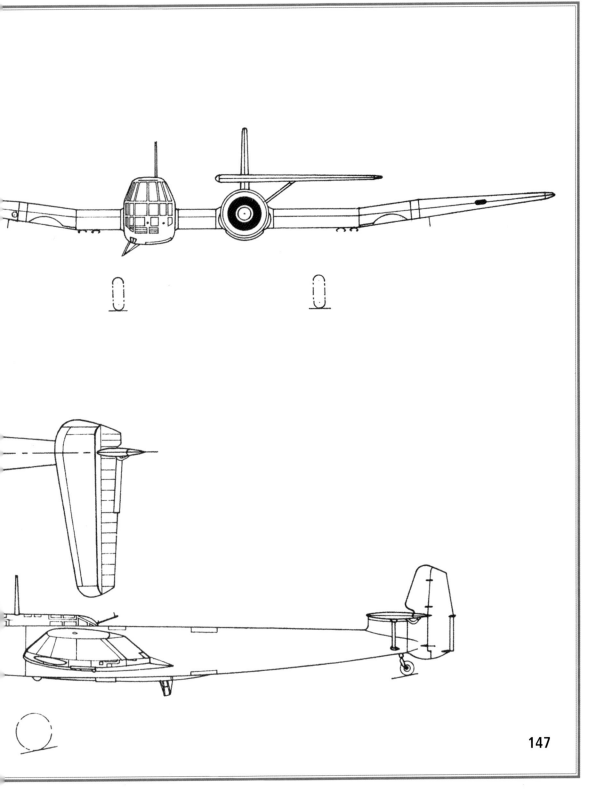

BRISTOL TYPE 167 BRABAZON

Kind of a Drag

That unusual name came from Lord Brabazon of Tara's 1943 committee to chart Great Britain's needs for post-World War II aviation. A result of the committee's findings, the Brabazon emerged as the world's largest airliner in its day--bigger even than the Boeing B-52. Meant for intercontinental travel, the Type 167 came equipped with eight engines driving eight propellers, but those propellers were in four sets of two contra-rotating props. Its range, 5,500 miles, outdistanced America's Lockheed Super Constellation and the Douglas DC-7. The airplane put the "luxury" in "airliner." It could transport 50 passengers, who might watch movies in its theater or have a drink in its cocktail lounge. Afterward they could nap in their own sleeping compartment. Even the six-man flight crew would be pampered within an inch of their lives: designers placed a spacious crew compartment behind the cockpit where the pilots, the flight engineers, the navigator or the radio operator could lounge or sleep while the Brabazon plied the skies. The designers also saw to it that the airliner would be equipped with the latest aerodynamic innovations. Just beneath the cockpit they included a gust response system, which detected turbulence and automatically compensated the airliner's controls for a smooth ride. On the tail they added large mass balances and hydraulics to make the elevators easy to manipulate. But such engineering forced them into some tradeoffs. Those balances, for instance, created a lot of drag, which kept the airplane's speed slower than it should have been. And the coupling of the engines meant that the wing had to be built thick, increasing drag even more. Though engineers started construction in 1945 the airplane first parted from the ground four years later-- the dawn of the Jet Age. And then fatigue cracks

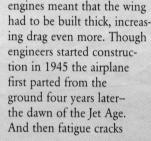

developed in the propeller mounts, so Britain's Air Registration Board refused to grant it unrestricted approval. Bristol built just one Brabazon, mainly because no one ordered any. All the airlines had their minds on jetliners. After spending 3 million pounds on the one and only Brabazon, Bristol broke the airliner up in 1953.

Bristol Type 167 Brabazon

Wingspan: 230 ft.
Length: 170 ft.
Height: 50 ft.
Maximum Speed: 300 m.p.h.
Maximum weight: 290,000 lbs.
Engines: eight 2,500 horsepower Bristol Centaurus radial engines
Construction: Aluminum

NORTHROP XP-56

Now this one had a Tail

The name: "Black Bullet." Northrop's XP-56 wasn't exactly a flying wing. It did have a bit of a fuselage, though most of the aft vertical stabilizer pointed downward. Meant as a cutting-edge fighter, the Black Bullet was driven by a 2,000 horsepower Pratt & Whitney R-2800 Double Wasp, typical of the times. The engine did drive two counter-rotating three-blade props in the aircraft's rear and the airplane incorporated the very first all-welded all-magnesium airframe. But pilots found it hard to handle. On one of the first taxi tests a tire blew and flipped the aircraft. Northrop built a second prototype XP-56 in 1944 with a bigger stabilizer and an improved wingtip design with a yaw control system. Testing revealed no significant performance improvement and the aircraft never entered production.

Right side view of Pratt & Whitney Double Wasp
R-2800 18-cylinder two-stage engine with downdrift
carburetor

Northrop XP-56
Wingspan: 27 ft. 6 in.
Height: 11 ft.
Max. Weight: 11,350 lbs.
Engine: Pratt & Whitney Double
Wasp
Max. Speed: 465 m.p.h.
(estimated).

DORNIER DO 335 PFIEL

Flying Anteater

Germany developed the Dornier Do 335 Pfiel (or "Arrow") late in the war. With its odd tractor/pusher engine combination, the name "Arrow" seemed a bit of misnomer: It really looked like an Anteater, which is what its Luftwaffe pilots called it. Like many warbirds that came out of Nazi Germany, the Do 335 came chock-full of innovations. For instance, the typical propeller twin has what's known as a "critical engine." If that engine dies, the airplane won't stay aloft for long. But the Do 335 had its engines mounted along the center line, which eliminated the critical engine problem as well as the divergent thrust typical of twins. Those two engines shot the Dornier along at a top speed of 475 miles per hour, nearly 20 mph faster than its Allied rival, the North American P-51 Mustang. The Do 335 did come equipped with a cruciform tail, and that, along with the spinning prop, might mince any pilot who

tried to bail out. So Dornier equipped the airplane with what was perhaps the first ejection seat on an operational aircraft. All he had to do was jettison the canopy—another innovative feature—then activate the ejection seat. To further increase his chance of survival (even during a belly landing) the pilot could pop off its vertical tail fins and the rear propeller. The Luftwaffe became so enamored with the Pfiel that it ordered a two-seat night-fighter version, which put a radar operator's seat behind and above the pilot's. Like many aircraft built by Germany late in the war the Do 335 program choked from lack of parts: 24-hour-a-day Allied bombing strangled the supply of engines, propellers, and radios, along with fuel. Yet it flew well. If the Nazis hadn't introduced the jet age at the very same time, more pusher/ tractor twins might have made their way into Allied Air Forces.

Dornier Do 335 Pfiel

Wingspan: 45 ft. 3 in.
Length: 45 ft. 5 in.
Height: 16 ft. 5 in.
Maximum weight: 22,000 lbs.
Maximum speed: 475 m.p.h.
Ceiling: 37,500 ft.
Range: 1,280 miles
Engines: Two 1,800-horsepower Daimler-Benz inverted V-12 piston engines

Underside of Dornier Do 335 Pfiel in flight

CURTISS-WRIGHT XP-55

America's First Swept-Wing Fighter

In 1939 the Army Air Corps had a new engine, the Pratt & Whitney X-1800, but it wanted an airplane developed around it and for it. In a fit of innovation the AAC put out a call for new aircraft that could be as unconventional as the designers wanted. Only thing: it had to have great visibility for the pilot, low drag characteristics, and, of course, killer weaponry. Curtiss-Wright's submission proved so unconventional that the Air Corps decided to reject it. But flush with funds from its successful P-40, Curtiss paid for a flying prototype of its submission. This, the XP-55, had winglets in the nose, swept wings in the back, and those wings placed aft of the pilot's seat for a great view. Along with the pusher engine (which they switched from the Pratt &

Whitney to an Allison), Curtiss engineers mounted the fighter on a retractable tricycle landing gear, a not-too-common configuration in those days. The first prototype crashed during stall tests in 1943. From further tests the following year the Army Air Force (hewed from the Army Air Corps in 1942) found out that the XP-55 didn't have much in the way of armament (four .50 caliber machine guns in the nose, compared with six in the wings of a contemporary fighter), it handled poorly at low speeds, and it wasn't so swift flying at top speeds either. The unconventional aircraft was abandoned, though its swept wing, tricycle gear and pusher engine found a home in nearly every jet airplane that followed.

Curtiss-Wright XP-55

Wingspan: 40 ft. 7 in.
Length: 29 ft. 7 in.
Height: 11 ft. 7 in.
Maximum weight: 7,929 lbs.
Top speed: 390 m.p.h.
Range: 635 miles
Weapons: four .50 caliber nose-mounted machine guns
Engine: One 1,275-horsepower Allison V-1710 inline piston engine

Bachem Ba 349 Natter

Rocket Nose

In the final days of the war Hitler approved any concept that might miraculously turn the war in his favor. One such plan was the Bachem Natter, a piloted missile made from plywood. Unskilled workers might have a problem with building wings, so ailerons were abandoned and all controls were in the elevators. The pilot was supposed to launch the Natter vertically, powered by four solid fuel rockets mounted on the sides and capable of 2,640-pounds of thrust each. After just 10 seconds the rockets would be released and within a minute reach 36,415 feet,—where the bombers were. Then the pilot would put it in a shallow dive, eject the covering on the nose and fire the 24 unguided missiles placed there. Then he'd dive

away from the bombers. The rest of the nose would fly off by releasing mechanical catches, then the pilot would be ejected by the deceleration of the aft fuselage, which had its own recovery chute to preserve the rocket engines. Meanwhile the pilot would pull his chute and float down to the ground. It sounded pretty desperate and it was:

In its first piloted vertical trial, in February 1945, test pilot Lothar Siebert was killed when the cockpit cover detached after launch. Still, today's F-15 can also fire rockets vertically—and shoot down spy satellites as they cruise overhead.

BACHEM BA 349 NATTER
Wingspan: 11 ft. 9 3/4 in
Length: 20 ft.
Max. Weight: 5,004 lbs.
Engine: 3,748 lb-thrust Walter rocket; four 2,640-lb-thrust Schmidding booster rockets.

NORTHROP XP-79

Flying Ginsu Knife

Northrop and the Army Air Force were so convinced that the flying wing would work that they tried anything to keep the flying wing shape flying. Take, for example, the XP-79 Flying Ram, built late in World War II. It was, of course, a flying wing, powered by two 1,400-pound-thrust Westinghouse Model B turbojets. It was also a fighter, but its attack mode now seems a bit unusual. It was designed to dive on enemy aircraft and slice them in two with its heavy-magnesium- and heavy-steel-armor plated wing. If that didn't work it might pepper the enemy aircraft with its four .50 caliber machine guns. Northrop guaranteed the Flying Ram for up to ten rams before it needed to be scrapped. The pilot lay prone, guaranteed to give him a neck ache. On its first flight in September 1945 it spun in and crashed. The pilot died, and then so did the program.

HARRY HUME CROSBY

Test pilot Harry Crosby flew the XP-79B for the first time on September 12, 1945. For fifteen minutes, it flew without problems but suddenly the plane went into a spin. Impossible to recover from, Crosby attempted to parachute out of the plane; his chute failed and he was killed. The XP-79B was destroyed by fire having impacted with the desert floor at Muroc Dry Lake in California.

Northrop XP-79

Wingspan: 38 ft.   **Length:** 14 ft.
Height: 7 ft. 6 in.   **Max. Speed:** 547 m.p.h. (estimated)
Engine: two Westinghouse 19B turbojets of 1,150 lbs. thrust each

YOKOSUKA MXY7 OHKA

One-Way Rocket Ride

The Yokosuka MXY7 Ohka was a great idea as far as rocket planes went. The Japanese built 755 of them by March 1945, and they were all built from non-strategic materials and were incredibly easy to fly. The pilot was to glide them then punch the rockets for a high speed approach to the target. There is no data on the landing characteristics of the Ohka (cherry blossom), for the ones that reached their targets exploded on impact. They were suicide planes, carrying 2,646 pounds of high explosives in the nose. Few actually reached the ships they were intended to hit, however; the launch vehicle, 16 Mitsubishi G4M2e twin-engine Bettys, tended to be destroyed by U.S. fighters before nearing the targets. They still released the Ohka, which usually nosed into the ocean. One did make it to a ship: the destroyer USS *Mannert L. Abele*, which sunk as a result of a direct hit in April 1945. By then production had ceased on the suicide plane; the Japanese deemed the converted bomber too slow to near the targets.

Yokosuka MXY7 Ohka [1945]
Wingspan: 16 ft. 9.5 in.
Length: 19 ft. 11 in.
Height: 3 ft. 9.75 in.
Weight: 4,718 lbs.
Engine: three solid propellant rockets;
combined thrust of 1,765 lbs.
Speed: 404 mph/range 23 miles.

Yokosuka MXYZ Ohka supported by a metal stand,
probably on exhibit at an airshow in the United States
shortly after WWII

HORTEN HO IX (GOTHA GO 229)

Earliest Stealth Jet

In a corner of a dark hangar filled with dusty aircraft at the National Air and Space Museum's Garber Restoration Facility in Silver Springs, Maryland, sits an odd, six-sided airfoil with a tricycle gear, two jet engines and an interesting tale behind it. In the last days of World War II the Horten brothers proposed to the Luftwaffe their Ho IX flying wing as a night fighter. This two-seater (for pilot and radar operator) was built with a combination of available, inexpensive tubular steel frame covered with plywood. And plywood is almost invisible to radar. It had a Junkers Jumo jet engine on either side of the

cockpit, which, like the B-2 stealth bomber, ended well before the wing's trailing edge—thus cooling the exhaust to make it invisible from the ground. It came equipped with two ejection seats inside the pressurized armored cabin. Estimated speed was 590 miles per hour. In other words, it was virtually a stealth bomber only about 40 years ahead of time. The airplane was partially built when Allied troops overran the Horten's assembly facility, and today it awaits restoration at the Garber facility.

Horten Ho IX (Gotha Go 229)
Wing Surface: 55.97 sq. yd.
Max. Weight: 16,519.8 lbs.
Engine: two 1,980-lb-thrust turbojets

Left side view of Horten Ho IX V3 jet flying wing. Outer wing panels are removed. Photo taken at Freeman Field ATSC, Seymore, Indiana

HUGHES H-4 HERCULES

The Spruce Goose

This airplane grew famous for not flying. Well, it did fly once. Designed in 1944 by the company of eccentric multimillionaire aviator Howard Hughes to help transport troops for the invasion of Japan, the Hughes H-4 was the largest airplane of its day–and for three decades afterward. Built from non-strategic materials, mostly wood, the seaplane could carry up to 750 fully equipped troops or 154,000 pounds of cargo (loaded through two massive clamshell doors built in the nose) across 3,500 miles of ocean. In theory. Workers finally completed it (in a hanger in Culver Field, California, what was then the world's largest building) two years after peace was declared and after the government became disinterested because Hughes felt that a Senate investigation questioned his integrity. He even paid for the construction himself. Really, everything about the Hercules was huge. Its wings were longer than a football field, it had no fewer than eight Pratt & Whitney four-rowed radial engines (twice the horsepower of a B-29 Superfortress), and it could carry 14,000 gallons of gas in its 14 floor tanks. The

wings had enough space inside to allow crewmembers service the 3,000-horsepower Pratts during flight. The horizontal stabilizer's span measured longer than a B-17's wing. Even its flight deck was more spacious than a wartime DC-3's. Trucking the "Spruce Goose" over the roads from Culver City to 290-foot Long Beach Harbor dry dock meant that city workers had to dismantle all the streetlights along the route. And that was expensive. Once workers finally assembled the "Spruce Goose" Hughes himself said he would perform its taxi tests. Seeing it in action generated tons of media interest, so on November 2, 1947, Los Angeles Harbor filled with boats holding print reporters and camera crews. Eighteen flight engineers and flight test observers took their places while fifteen reporters and invited guests sat in airline-style seats. Then Hughes took the pilot's seat. He placed his right hand on the "Spruce Goose's" eight throttles, and gave it the gas. It moved over the water. Then Hughes requested 15 degrees of flap from the engineer–and that was the takeoff setting. Hughes poured on the fuel and when it reached

nearly 100 miles per hour the "Spruce Goose" skimmed the water's surface and—while thousands of jaws dropped—the airplane parted with the water and climbed. It reached an altitude of 80 feet, and after almost a mile Hughes chopped the power and the seaplane settled back to the surface. Hughes taxied the "Spruce Goose" back to its dock and the newsreels and papers reported its flight the next day. Hughes had thumbed his nose at the Senate. His workers towed it into a nearby hangar and for decades Hughes paid well for its maintenance. Until his death in the early 1970s he could have wandered into that hangar and taken it out for another joyride. After he died the airplane, along with the luxury liner Queen Mary, became a Long Beach tourist attraction. Ultimately Washington State's Evergreen Air Museum bought the "Spruce Goose", and today it's on display there, dwarfed only by the Lockheed C-5A Galaxy and the Antonov An 225.

"It's a 'Spruce Goose.' It'll never fly."
—Senate Investigative Committee

Hughes H-4 Hercules
Wingspan: 320 ft.
Length: 219 ft.
Height: 79 ft.
Top speed: 175 m.p.h. (estimated)
Range: 3,500 miles
Weight: 400,000 lbs. fully loaded
Engines: eight 3,000-horsepower Pratt & Whitney R-4360 28-cylinder radials

Hughes H-4 Hercules 'Spruce Goose' being towed by tugboat out of the Los Angeles harbor on November 2nd, 1949 in prepration for its take-off run

BELL RP-63A KINGCOBRA

Bullets Just Bounced off

During World War II the United States Army Air Force decided that live-fire exercises against banners towed by aircraft lacked reality. So 300 Bell RP-63 Kingcobras were built for use in live fire exercises. The gunners of other aircraft would go gunning straight for the Kingcobras. Its guns were removed, and oddly enough all armor was also removed from the aircraft. Yet all external surfaces—the wings, fuselage, tail, etc.—received an extra layer of an alloy called duraluminum weighing some 1,500 pounds. They also added bulletproof glass on every inch of the canopy, included a thick-walled prop, and bolted on a steel grill over the air intake and exhaust. The gunners used frangible bullets, and when they scored a hit a red light blinked. While the USAAF never flew the RP-63 as a pilotless drone, today we do fire live weapons such as Sidewinder missiles on old fighter jets flown from the ground. Otherwise warbirds are equipped with the electronics to tell when a pilot has scored or taken a hit. A current fighter just costs too much to shoot down.

Bell RP-63A Kingcobra
Wingspan: 38 ft. 4 in.
Length: 32 ft. 8 in.
Max. Weight: 12,000 lbs.
Engine: 1,325 horsepower
Allison 12-cylinder
inline V

Low right side aerial view of U.S. Air
Force Bell RP-63A Kingcobra in flight

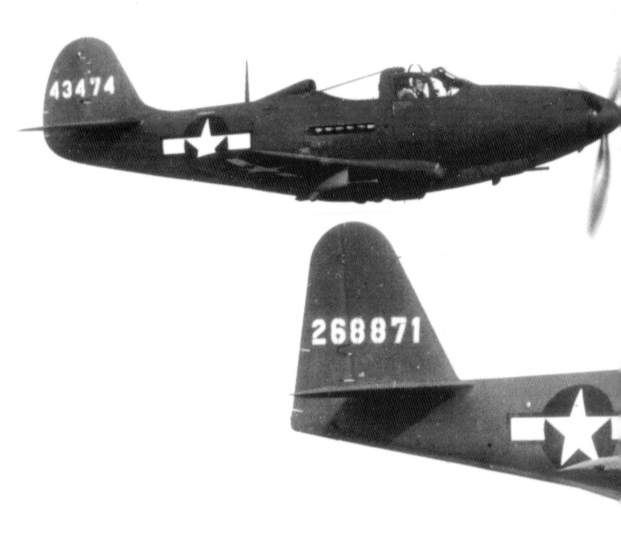

The right side view of Bell P-39Q Airacobra (top, s/n 44-3474) in flight in formation with Bell P-63A Kingcobra (bottom, s/n 42-68871).

MESSERSCHMITT ME 163 KOMET

The first rocket-powered airplane

Nazi Germany always pushed the outer edge of the envelope. In 1939 Dr. Alexander Lippisch, who designed the DFS 194 tail-less glider, brought his concept and his team to the Messerschmitt company and immediately set to work building the swept-wing Me 163 rocket plane. At the Nazi's secret rocket base at Peenemunde an Me 110 towed the first engineless prototype into the air, and in the summer of 1941 they installed a Walter

1,653-pound-thrust rocket engine, fueled by hydrogen peroxide and hydrazine/methanol. The design team clocked the rocket plane at 550 miles per hour, around 150 miles per hour faster than a piston-engine fighter. It was a small machine and had little space for conventional landing gear, so it shot into the air on a trolley and landed on a retractable skid. Also, its fuel, known as "T-stoff," lasted just 7 minutes and 30 seconds, and it was incredibly caustic, forcing the ground crew to don protective rubber suits during refueling. Plus, it was highly unstable. Twice during tests the T-stoff exploded, each time flattening a building. On the more positive side laborers could construct the Me 163 from wood and it climbed at 16,400 feet per minute, only about 3,000 fpm slower than a modern F-15. Equipped with two 30-millimeter cannon, the Komet could shoot upward, shoot down an American bomber and glide back to base. Pilots didn't kill many bombers, however: in its time the Me 163's were too much for

pilots acclimated to piston fighters. Postwar, the U.S. took a few home and analyzed them and built the rocket-powered rocket-powered Bell X-1, in which Chuck Yeager flew faster than the speed of sound. One of its ancestors, the X-15, climbed so high that the Air Force bestowed astronaut wings on a few of its pilots.

Messerschmitt Me 163 Komet

Wingspan: 30 ft. 6.125 in.
Length: 17 ft. 9.375 in.
Height: 9 ft.
Top Speed: 600 m.p.h.
Empty Weight: 4,191 lbs.
Max. Weight: 9,061 lbs.
Max. Speed: 596 m.p.h.
Engines: Walter HWK 509A-1 or A-2 rocket with 3,748 lbs. thrust

McDonnell XP-85 Goblin

Goblin? Try Parasite

In 1945, in an effort to secure more protection for bombers during bombing missions, engineers came up with the idea of attaching a fighter to the bomber, then release it to do battle against swarms of enemy fighters coming from enemy airfields. One of these was the XP-85 Goblin, built by McDonnell Aircraft Corporation. The Goblin was a chubby, slightly over 14 feet long swept-wing jet fighter. It had winglets, and four tail planes. Suspended and captured by a nose hook, the Goblin was supposed to battle the aggressors in-between. Two were built. The so-called parasite airplanes were tested on the B-29. After two hours of tests engineers found that the fighter was slow and unmaneuverable compared with the fighters it was supposed to intercept, plus bomber turbulence made the parasite difficult to land and takeoff. And then someone else came up with a better idea: in-flight refueling. With a tanker circling overhead just out of enemy range, friendly fighters could refuel and accompany bombers all the way to their targets. Both Goblins survived, one in the Air Force Museum in Dayton, Ohio; and the other at Offutt Air Force Base in Omaha, Nebraska.

McDonnell XP-85 Goblin
Wingspan: 21 ft. 1.5 in.
Engine: 3,000-lb-thrust Westinghouse
J34 turbojet

Three-quarter left front view of McDonnell XP-85 Goblin from low angle on ground handling dolly

CONVAIR XF2Y-1 SEA DART

Wet and Wild

For some reason the Navy wanted a fighter that could land and take off from the sea, instead of from an aircraft carrier. In 1951 it awarded a contract to Convair, builder of the more conventional land-based F-102 Delta Dagger and later the F-106 Delta Dart, to construct the Convair XF2Y-1 Sea Dart. A prototype jet hydroplane fighter, the Sea Dart would run along the watery surface until it picked up enough speed to rise on its two skis, then aquaplane until it had enough speed to takeoff. To prevent water from drowning its two jet engines, they were mounted on the fighter's back. The prototype, however, performed poorly, what with the vibrations caused by the skis. But one managed to go supersonic in a dive. Convair built only two Sea Darts before the Navy cancelled the contract in 1956.

182

Convair XF2Y-1 Sea Dart [1951]
Wingspan: 38 ft. 8 in.
Length: 52 ft. 7 in.
Height: 20 ft. 9 in.
Max weight: 16,527 lbs.
Engines: two 6,000-lb-thrust Westinghouse J46 turbojets with afterburners.
Max speed: 695 m.p.h. estimated.

RYAN X-13 VERTIJET

Takes off Vertically, Lands...Well...

Fantasy author Ray Bradbury likes to have his silvery rockets land tail-first on Mars and then astronauts emerge and run into some amazing adventure. This type of landing just doesn't work well here on earth. Engineers designed the 10,000-pound-thrust Ryan X-13 to take off suspended vertically from a ground trailer. And that it did: the first prototype got off the ground in December 1955–taking off and landing soon after, on its tricycle gear. It flew pretty well. The second prototype completed the transition from horizontal to vertical flight in 1957, but such tail-first landings were deemed too difficult for pilots to perform. Maybe the Earth's gravity is too strong. Astronauts landed on the moon in the Lunar Module–a VTOL lander–and emerged into some amazing adventure. Much like Ray Bradbury said they would.

Ryan X-13 Vertijet

Wingspan: 21 ft.
Length: 24 ft.
Max Weight: 7,500 lbs.
Engine: 10,000 lb-thrust Rolls-Royce Avon turbojet

TEST 7-B
1-25-51

Left side view of Ryan X-13 Vertijet experimental VTOL aircraft mounted on its ground service trailer which has been raised to a 45 degree angle.

TAYLOR AEROCAR MODEL I

It Drives! It Flies! It Drives!

To paraphrase veteran aviation journalist Richard L. Collins, 'You can't make a car that flies like an airplane, and you can't make an airplane that drives like a car.' And yet since the first hybrid–the Curtiss Autoplane–so many people have tried to do just that. The late '40s vintage Aerocar was a bit different from the Curtiss machine: it could tow itself around.

Designed by Molton Taylor of Longview, Washington, the Aerocar was a compact automobile–Volkswagen size–powered by a 150-horsepower Lycoming engine. Instead of the wheels being buried inside of wheelwells, the four wheels stuck out like landing gear. But otherwise it resembled a car. All the operator had to do was back the Aerocar into the easily assembled wings and Y-tail (from which the propeller protruded via a long, long extension shaft), attach it good and tight, and take off from any local runway. Once he landed at another runway far away he could pull the "airplane" over to the taxi strip, detach the wings and tail and fold them into a compact package, and tow them around until it was time to take off again. Then he drove off to the airport, reassembled the wings and tail, bolted the car and airplane parts together, and flew back home. Taylor built seven over the next seven years, and finally received FAA certification in 1956. But the auto was too small, the concept of assembling both major components into a plane too tenuous, to ever develop a market. And perhaps, like Collins says, you can't make a car that flies like an airplane, and you can't make an airplane that drives like a car. Today, though, you can see the stylish, elegant Aerocar at the Experimental Aircraft Association's annual convention in Oshkosh, Wisconsin. It's a rare bird–er, hybrid.

MOLTON TAYLOR

Taylor Aerocar Model I

Wingspan: 30 ft.

Length (as airplane): 21 ft.

Height (as airplane): 7 ft. 2 in.

Length of car: 10 ft. 4 in.

Length of trailer: 8 ft.

Width of trailer: 13 ft.

Max. Weight: 2,100 lbs.

Empty Weight: 1,300 lbs.

Engine: Lycoming 0-320, 4-cylinder, horizontally opposed, rated at 150 horsepower

Max. Speed: 110 m.p.h.

View of Aerocar, Inc. Model I (r/n N31214) in roadable configuration (wings and rear fuselage folded into trailer mode) parked on snowy ground outside the Aerocar, Inc. plant at Longview, Washington, circa 1949-1950

CONVAIR X-6

Watch the Passengers Glow

After Hiroshima nuclear engineers experimented with ways to use nuclear reactors for peaceful purposes. By 1951 the US Air Force engaged in the Aircraft Nuclear Propulsion program, which would explore the possibility of building airplanes capable of propulsion by clean, safe, nuclear energy—and stay aloft almost forever. It seemed like a great idea under the threat of nuclear attack from the Soviet Union. The power plant itself weighed a total of 140,000 pounds, which included the reactor shielding. The flight crew sat inside 24,000 pounds of crew shielding. The designers originally wanted the reactor to operate at 2,500 degrees F, but no known aviation material could contain that kind of heat. So they opted for 1,800 degrees. But as it turned out, they would have to shield the reactor on the ground lest some unsuspecting ground crew walk by and become irradiated. And if the bomber crashed on US soil the radiation would be spread for who knows how far, killing who knows how many. Ultimately the Air Force canceled the X-6 program in 1953, before the first one could be

built. While nuclear powered aircraft proved unfeasable, such experiments helped lead to aircraft that could stay up longer and fly farther than the piston-powered aircraft prevalent around the same time as the X-6.

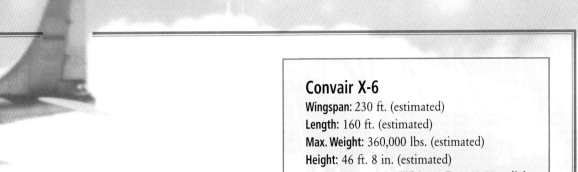

Convair X-6

Wingspan: 230 ft. (estimated)
Length: 160 ft. (estimated)
Max. Weight: 360,000 lbs. (estimated)
Height: 46 ft. 8 in. (estimated)
Engine: Six Pratt & Whitney R-4360-53 radials of 3,800 hp. each (takeoff power) and four General Electric J47-GE-19 turbojets of 5,200 lbs. thrust each

Consolidated NB-36H Peacemaker (s/n 51-5712) airborne nuclear reactor test bed in flight over cloud layer. A Boeing B-50 chase plane at top

McDonnell F3H-1 Demon

A Demon to the Navy

To counter the Russian MiG-15 dominating the Korean skies in the early 1950s, the U.S. Navy ordered the McDonnell F-3 Demon into production even before its XF-3 prototype had lifted off the runway. And the Navy even ordered 100 Demons to be built under license by the Temco Aircraft Corporation, Dallas, Texas. It was to be powered by the Westinghouse J40-WE-22, which developed 10,900 pounds per thrust with afterburning, but that still left the F-3 underpowered. The first Demon was sent to the Navy's test center at Patuxent River, Maryland. Not only was the airplane underpowered, its engine was given to sudden failure and inflight explosion. Within a short period the F-3 had 11 major accidents, many fatal.

McDonnell F3H-1 Demon
Wingspan: 35 ft. 4 in.
Length: 58 ft. 11 in.
Max. Weight: 33,971 lbs.
Height: 14 ft. 7 in.
Engine: 10,900 lb-thrust (with afterburner)
Westinghouse J40 turbojet
Max. Speed: 618 m.p.h.

SNECMA VTOL

Sucks the Pilot Right In

In 1952-53 SNECMA, a French company, took a big, barrel-shape wing and stuffed a 99-pound-thrust pulse jet engine in it. That machine got off the ground in 1954, remote-controlled and tethered. So excited were the French that they built another larger remote-controlled test vehicle, this time with a 6,393-pound-thrust turbojet inside a vertical nacelle. The whole device sat on four castored wheels. It first flew in September of 1956, followed by some 205 test flights—all of them tethered. This led to the C.400 P-2, which now included an ejection seat and a pilot. By 1958 it had flown 123 successful flights, some tethered and some free. Giddy with success, SNECMA now built the C.450-01, which took off vertically and successfully in May 1959. But three months later the pilot tried to transition from vertical to horizontal flight and the "airplane" spun out of control. The pilot ejected safely and lived to fly another day, the machine crashed and the project died.

SNECMA VTOL

Engine: 7,716 lb-thrust
Altar 101E
turbojet

THE GOODYEAR INFLATOPLANE

Doubles as an Inflatable Mattress

The 1950s seemed rife with possibility. Every product that came out had one of those smooth optimistic names that positively reeked of the wonderful, easy life that would result from that product alone: The Instamatic Camera, The Hydroflow Transmission, The Goodyear Inflatoplane. Designed and built in just 12 weeks by Goodyear engineers in 1952, the Inflatoplane was essentially a flying inner tube. Its secret was a patented material known as Airmat, which consisted of two layers of rubberized nylon fabric "connected by drop threads that hold [these] surfaces a fixed difference apart under internal pressure," according to a contemporary Goodyear brochure. Varying the length of those drop threads showed the engineers exactly what different shapes they could make. And one of those shapes turned out to be an airfoil for wings and tail surfaces. The finished Inflatoplane had a length of 20 feet and a wingspan of 22 feet. It took just 10 minutes for the Inflatoplane to be blown up by the same 44-horsepower engine that propelled it through the air. It resembled a blimp, with blimp-like wings. But without any helium on board. The all rubber airplane could fold up into a small package–five feet per side–and it weighed just 200 pounds. A sweet concept: store it in your garage, inflate it in the driveway, fly off to work in the morning then fly back in the evening. According to the manufacturer, with a pilot on board and a full tank of gas it weighed 550 pounds, took off in 300 feet, and cruised at 60 miles per hour for 6.5 hours. What's more, according to *Janes All the World's Aircraft*, it could remain inflated and flying even when riddled with .30 caliber bullets. Which reveals one more customer that Goodyear hoped would come shopping: The U.S. Government. The military could drop an Inflatoplane to a downed U.S. pilot, who could inflate it in 10 minutes and be on his way, hopefully, before the enemy arrived.

So how did it perform? "Not too well," says Bill Turner, who Goodyear assigned to the Inflatoplane project, and who now heads Repeat Aircraft in Riverside, California. In high winds the Inflatoplane would wobble. In the air it was unstable. Turner says he spent most of his time on the project talking to the engineer. On the ground. "I didn't get to be an old, old, bold pilot by doing dumb things in the air," Turner says. Goodyear built 12 Inflatoplanes before it decided to stick to tires and blimps. The company tried to revive the idea in 1971, but like the first version this old soldier quietly faded away.

"I saw it attempt to fly, but it wasn't rigid enough. And it flew too slowly. Any kind of wind and it would fly backwards. It wasn't that easy to assemble and if you assembled it wrong you might get killed. Even if you assembled it right you might." –Bill Turner

The Goodyear Inflatoplane

Wingspan: 22 ft.
Length: 20 ft.
Empty Weight: 240 lbs.
Engine: 44-horsepower two-stroke, 4-cylinder Nelson engine.
Top Speed: 72 m.p.h.

**GA-447 with new wing design (span: 34'0")
for military evaluation ca. 1956**

ROGALLO WING

More Fun than Playing in Sand

The Russians landed their crewed space capsules on land, and the Americans landed theirs in the ocean. The American way was more expensive (it required a Navy ship and a few helicopters and frogmen, etc.) so an engineer for NASA named Francis Rogallo came up with a solution. Known as the Rogallo Wing, it would unfold on a Gemini spacecraft after it reentered the atmosphere and would act as a parachute and allow the crew to land on U.S. soil. The Wing was more simple than a cardboard box. It consisted of four parts: three lightweight tubes, one running down the middle dissecting a broad V-shape made from the outer two. Its cover consisted of a loose, lightweight nylon cloth that ballooned outward as the wing flew, creating lift similar to that of a modern sport parachute. With the capsule attached somewhere near the middle the simple device would allow the capsule to glide down and land presumably under the crews' control. It never caught on with NASA, however, but in the late 60s it spawned a movement that still exists today. That's right: hang gliding. As time flew by such gliders became more complex, with ribs and two-surface wings more swept than delta. And today Francis Rogallo is revered by glider fliers everywhere as the father of, yes, hang gliding.

FRANCIS ROGALLO

The Rogallo Foundation was formed in 1992, and the foundation now plans to construct a museum close to the Wright Brothers Memorial on North Carolina's Outer Banks. Dedicated to Francis and Gertrude Rogallo, the museum will preserve their papers, research and artifacts.

Rogallo Wing
Wingspan: 31 ft.
Stall Speed: up to 20 m.p.h.

RYAN XV-8A FLEEP

A Jeep that Flew

In 1963 Ryan, famous for building the *Spirit of Saint Louis* back in 1927, concocted a flexible-wing aircraft that would fly around and then land and drive around like a jeep. This predecessor to the ultra-light category had a fabric Rogallo wing with an inflatable leading edge; the cockpit, a pod-like affair, hung beneath it. Its engine was a pusher, and it rested on a tricycle gear. Best of all it could fold up into a small package. Nothing much came out if it except an unusual nickname: Fleep, for Flying Jeep. In the end, the project was cancelled and its V-8 designation went to the Hawker Harrier.

Ryan XV-8A Fleep

Wingspan: 33 ft. 5 in.
Length: 19 ft. 6 in.
Payload: 1,185 lbs.
Max. Speed: 67 m.p.h. (estimated)
Engine: 210-horsepower Continental IO-360

CONVAIR XFY-1 POGO

Don't Forget to Look Over your Shoulder

Here's another airplane designed to sit on its tail, and fly from the confined decks of smaller ships. It looked like a yard dart with four small, castoring wheels attached to the fins. Counter-rotating props propelled this early 1950s Navy design, and in 1954 James F. "Skeets" Coleman completed the first tethered takeoff and landing. By November of that same year they had worked up to transition from vertical to horizontal flight and then back to vertical. But it experienced major control problems, and it initially remained near San Diego, but in the early-to mid-60's, the Navy shipped it to Naval Air Station Norfolk, Virginia. In 1973, it was moved to a museum, the National Air & Space Museum. Today vertical takeoff and land remains the realm of helicopters.

JAMES F. COLEMAN

Built to protect shipping convoys, the Pogo sat on a ship's deck housed against the saltwater in its own conical hangar.

Convair XFY-1 Pogo

Wingspan: 27 ft. 7.75 in.
Length: 34 ft. 11.75 in.
Max. weight: 16,250 lbs.
Engine: 5,850 horsepower Allison turboprop driving coaxial contrarotating propellers.
Max speed: 610 m.p.h.

View from high angle of Convair XFY-1 (Pogo) on the ground in position for vertical takeoff

205

Curtiss-Wright X-19 VTOL

A Helicopter and Airplane Rolled into One

Among the dreams of commuters and soldiers alike is a craft that takes off like a helicopter and then flies like an airplane, then switches back to helicopter mode for landing. They're called tilt rotors, and they're easier to describe than build successfully. Around 1960 Curtiss-Wright stuck its toes in the tilt-rotor water. Called the X-100, it was a single-seater proof-of-concept aircraft that had a single 825-horsepower turboprop buried in the fuselage and driving the two tilting rotors situated on either winglet. The turboprop also provided thrust through a controllable tail nozzle to keep the tiltrotor aloft at low speeds and during rotor transitions from horizontal to vertical and vice-versa. It didn't fly all that great, but the honchos at Curtiss-Wright thought it

flew well enough to build a bigger tilter, the X-19. In fact, the company even received a contract from the Air Force for two six-seat X-19s. Each X-19 came with two tandem wings and four 13-foot tilting prop-rotors on each wingtip; each had two 2,200-horsepower Lycoming turboprops cleverly cross-shafted so that one turboprop could drive all four props in case an engine died. The company only delivered one X-19 to the Air Force, and that one didn't fly well. Its first flight was on June 26, 1964; its last was August 25, 1965. That was the day it crashed. Lately Boeing had more success with its V-22, though the Marines investigated the craft after two crashes that killed everyone on board.

Curtiss-Wright X-19 VTOL

Wingspan: front 20 ft.
back 20 ft. 11 in.
Length: 41 ft.
Height: 20 ft. 7 in.
Max. weight: 13,580 lbs.
Max. speed: 406 m.p.h.
Engines: two 2,200-horsepower
Lycoming T-55-5 engines

RHEIN-FLUGZEUGBAU FANTRAINER 600

Watch on the Rhein

Pilots learned that the big problem with piston engine aircraft is torque: the propeller wants to turn the airplane to the right. Fighter jets don't have this tendency to turn right; they stay where the pilot points the nose. And that's good. Fighter jocks have to worry a lot more about dogfighting and bomb dropping than they do flying the airplane. So with that concept in mind Rhein-Flugzeugbau designed its Fantrainer 600, a fighter trainer with little if any divergent thrust. First flown in 1977, the tandem cockpit trainer had a ducted fan mounted just behind the forward swept wing. Aside from nearly eliminating torque, ducted fans (that consists of a multi-blade propeller that spins inside a close-fitting

duct) reduce noise, fuel consumption, and air pollution. To keep airflow from interfering with the tail, it was mounted on top of the rudder—a T-tail, in other words. Plus, it had retractable gear.

Overall the Fantrainer looked unusual, but sleek. Despite that, only one country bought it: the Royal Thai Air Force took delivery of just 16 600s. Receiving most of those as kits, the Thais assembled them and found that their composite structures refuse to deteriorate in the jungle. Other nations tested the trainer, however, and called it underpowered. But Thailand seems contented, and uses the 600 to train pilots in the country's Northrop F-5s.

Rhein-Flugzeugbau Fantrainer 600
Wingspan: 31 ft. 10 in.
Length: 31 ft. 2 in.
Height: 9 ft. 10 in.
Max. Weight: 5,060 lbs.
Max. Speed: 258 m.p.h.
Engine: One 650-horsepower Allison 250 turboshaft driving a five-blade Hoffman fan

NASA/Ames AD-1

A One-Piece Swiveling Wing

The so-called variable-geometry wing–used to decrease take-off and landing speeds, increasing cruise and maximum speeds in flight, and reduce fuel burn–arose in baby steps. The carrier-based F-8 Crusader came with a wing that rose upward; the Air Force F-111's wing swept forward and then backward. Same with the Navy Grumman F-14. Those were production airplanes. In 1978 NASA and Ames Industrial Corporation made the experimental AD-1 to test an evolution of variable geometry. The jet's entire wing pivoted. The oblique wing, an idea conceived by Ames Research Center

Aeronautical Engineer Robert T. Jones, with detailed design by Burt Rutan, was built from composite materials like most of his airplanes–the jet's wing swept forward up to 60 degrees. Aside from the wing innovation, the cockpit was narrow and compact, but long enough for the pilot to stretch out. Those who flew it found it comfortable, and added that the AD-1 handled fine. NASA called the project useful for research, and even studied the oblique wing for future jetliners and fighter planes. Budget restrictions led the agency away from the innovative concept.

NASA/Ames AD-1

Wingspan: 32 ft.; **Oblique:** 16 ft. 2 in.
Length: 38 ft. 9 in.
Height: 6 ft. 9 in.
Maximum weight: 2,000 lbs.
Maximum speed: 170 m.p.h.
Engine: Two 153-pound-thrust Ames Industrial turbojets

Concept illustration of the NASA/Ames AD-1

GLOSSARY

Ace: A pilot who shoots down five airplanes (or, in World War I, balloons). Early in the war stunt-flier-turned-fighter-pilot Rolland Garros shot down an astonishing five enemy airplanes (with a machine gun that fired through the propeller) before being shot down himself. The next person to reach that number was christened an "ace," the highest card in the deck.

Aileron: Wing surfaces in which one swivels upward while the other swivels downward and vice-versa. Used for turning or leveling an aircraft.

Airfoil: A form designed to provide lift.

Amphibian: Like its namesake, the amphibious aircraft operates either on water or solid terra firma. This metamorphosis is usually due to retractable landing gear.

Anhedral: Opposite of Dihedral, literally. The wings of an aircraft sag or drop in an inverted-V or -U shape.

Biplane: An airplane with two wings, usually placed one on top of another.

Camber: The curvature of a wing.

Canard: French, for, literally, duck. The animal, not the action. Such an aircraft's wing is mounted aft, with its horizontal stabilizer placed forward.

Cantilever: A wing that supports its own weight and needs no external bracing.

Counter-rotating propellers: Propellers that spin in opposite directions. For many reasons a propeller turns an airplane in the direction it's spinning. Having one propeller that spins in the opposite direction counteracts that effect.

Cruciform: Cross-shape.

Elevator: Movable horizontal surface for directing the aircraft's nose up or down.

Empennage: The aft part of the fuselage, which usually includes the horizontal and vertical stabilizer.

Envelope: To draw an aircraft's performance chart, test pilots determine how fast the aircraft can safely fly at specific altitudes up to its determined ceiling. This chart forms a rough rectangle or a parallelogram, much like an envelope. To "fly the outside edge of the envelope," "push the envelope," "hang your butt over the edge," a pilot flies faster or higher than graphed on the performance chart. This is not a recommended practice--except in an emergency.

Floatplane: An airplane that can only land or takeoff on water. Also known as a Seaplane.

Fuselage: Placed perpendicular to the wing, it's French for Spindle.

Horizontal stabilizer: The horizontal member used to stabilize an aircraft, which may or not have the elevator attached.

H-tail: A tail with its horizontal and vertical stabilizers forming capital H. See also T-tail.

In-line engine: Powerplant with all its cylinders in a row.

Monoplane: An aircraft with one horizontal lifting surface--though it may be interrupted by the fuselage.

Multiplane: An aircraft with more than three wings.

Ornothopter: An aircraft whose wing is designed to flap. Thus far no human-carrying ornithopter exist except in fiction.

Parasite: A fighter attached to a larger, slower aircraft, often meant to be released and do battle with attacking forces over enemy territory and thus beyond the range of friendly fighters.

Pusher: A propeller or engine-propeller combination positioned pointed aft, so that its thrust pushes the airplane. See also Tractor.

Radial engine: A piston engine with its cylinders mounted in a flat circle facing forward. Radials tend to have an odd number of cylinders so they won't have annoying vibrations. Usually cooled by air, since they face into the oncoming air.

Rib: Fore-and-aft wing member designed to give the airfoil its shape and the wing its strength.

Rag, or Rag wing: An airplane of fabric-covered wood.

Rotary engine: A radial engine where the crankshaft is bolted in place, and thus the cylinders remain stationary and the crankcase moves. The propeller is bolted directly to the crankcase. The spinning helps cool the engine, but the crankcase's weight also produces a gyroscopic effect. Many World War I fighters were so-equipped, and that allowed them to turn in a flash. so it was great for dogfights. But rotary engine machines were highly unstable in takeoffs, so the pilot had to be alert--and skilled.

Rudder: Movable vertical surface used to help steer the airplane left or right, much like a ship.

Rudder pedals: Pedals under pilot's feet used to activate the rudder left or right, depending on which foot the pilot presses.

Spar: Longitudinal or spanwise member running inside a wing or control surface. Not only provides a place upon which to attach the ribs, but also gives the wing strength.

Stall: Has nothing to do with the engine dying. Absolutely nothing. A stall is an aerodynamic condition that occurs when the wing no longer generates lift.

Stick: Control between pilot's leg, held by same, and used to activate the control surfaces such as the elevator and ailerons. Pushing forward lowers the nose, pulling back raises the nose, moving left turns airplane left, moving right turns airplane right. The British call it joystick. See also Yoke.

Tractor: A propeller or engine-propeller combination positioned pointed forward, so that its thrust pulls the airplane. See also Pusher.

Triplane: An aircraft with three wings.

T-tail: A tail with its horizontal stabilizer positioned on top of its vertical stabilizer, forming a capital T. See also H-tail.

Yoke: A half steering wheel used to control the airplane. See Stick.

INDEX

217